Tom Joseph has finally captured the essence of "being stuck" in various areas of our lives, a condition which holds us back from fulfilling the greatness God put within us. I truly believe the work Tom is doing will revolutionize our mindset, allowing us to see things as they really are rather than as we want them to be. He has done a masterful job of explaining the often-complicated issues that cause us to get "stuck." Because he makes them easier to understand, he also makes them easier to overcome, drastically changing our everyday walk with both God and man.

Read *Why We Stay Stuck*, and you too can live a life that is the full expression of the potential within you.

- Dr. W.T. Bolan D.C.

Why We Stay Stuck

Tom Joseph MA, L.C.P.C.

Licensed Clinical Pastoral Counselor

CrossHouse

Published by
CrossHouse Publishing
PO Box 461592
Garland, TX 75046-1592
Copyright Tom Joseph 2007
All Rights Reserved
Printed in the United States of America
by Lightning Source, LaVergne, TN
Cover design by Dennis Davidson
Except where otherwise indicated, all Scripture taken from the
King James Version

ISBN: 0-929292-72-3
Library of Congress Control Number: 2007931814

TO ORDER ADDITIONAL COPIES FOR $14.95 EACH
(ADD $3 SHIPPING FOR FIRST BOOK,
50 CENTS FOR EACH ADDITIONAL BOOK)
CONTACT CROSSHOUSE PUBLISHING
PO BOX 461592
GARLAND, TX 75046-1592
www.crosshousepublishing.org
877-212-0933 (toll-free)

Foreword

After Tom Joseph took the platform and began to speak, it was quickly evident that this would not be your run-of-the-mill presentation on codependency. As one who had been an alcoholic by age 20 and who then had worked in the arena of substance abuse, I had a clear understanding of codependent indications. Yet in my own Christian counseling practice, I had seen that Christians in particular tend to shrink from the idea that codependency could even vaguely apply to their relationships. In less than 90 minutes that day, Tom Joseph gave me and the other professional Christian counselors in the audience a real sense of hope.

Why We Stay Stuck clearly outlines the reasons the power of the family has been neutralized and in some cases disarmed in our society. It gives concrete evidence for how the religious ideology of our day has led people to tolerate, and even disregard, the abusive nature of those with whom they are significantly engaged relationally.

Matthew 24:12 says, "And because iniquity will abound, the love of many shall wax cold." Iniquity, or lawlessness, refers to the flagrant defiance of what is right or the setting aside of healthy boundaries put in place to protect people, whether in a marital relationship or in societies at large. In this verse, Jesus talks about a world in which man becomes his own idol. Watching out for number one seems to be epidemic today. It would be illusory to tell you that Christians are setting an example to the lawless. In fact, in most cases it seems difficult to see a definitive division between those who claim Christ as Savior and those who do not.

Tom Joseph is a clear voice in this world where love is growing cold. *Why We Stay Stuck* unambiguously lays out the signs and symptoms of unhealthy relationships with subsequent real-life stories of those Tom has helped. While his experience speaks volumes, it is his authenticity and candor that crystallize his effectiveness. *Why We Stay Stuck* unpretentiously cuts through our Christian façades, calling the issues what they are, and then outlining processes that will lead to resolution.

— Jeanne M. Kuckelman, M.S.
Licensed Clinical Christian Counselor

Acknowledgments

First, I must acknowledge the person who is really responsible for this book coming to fruition: my wife, Vicki. Vicki not only has been my greatest encourager and cheerleader, but she has also worked countless hours helping develop and write this book. She has juggled her schedule with the children, kept the house, and managed my counseling office in order to make *Why We Stay Stuck* happen.

Second, I thank my son Alex and my four step-children, Candice, and her husband Nick, Cassie, Steve and Luke, for being such good kids and making it possible for me to focus on writing.

And last, I want my friend Doug Groskopf to know how grateful I am for his support and constant encouragement throughout this project.

Table of Contents

Introduction

Far too many people stay stuck in circumstances that deprive them of the emotional, relational, and financial healing they so desperately need. How do I know this? From my varied experience in my family life counseling practice, hospital treatment centers, and the radio talk program that I host.

Also, I have personally dealt with many of the same relational and behavioral struggles that cause difficulties for those I counsel. I remember coming to the realization that, even though I longed for real change from the dysfunctional people in my own life, I was actually enabling them. So desperate was I to fix my circumstances that I said and did things that actually made them worse. The problem was, I didn't know then what was really wrong. I was fighting something I could neither see nor understand. What I needed was wisdom.

"Sophia" is the word the ancient Greeks used for wisdom. Their definition goes much like this: Wisdom is *that which can see the true nature of a thing.* I like that definition. Most people with behavioral and relational problems really don't have a clue about the true nature of their particular "thing." *Why We Stay Stuck* will reveal how to change your circumstances even though it appears nothing is working. And even if you're not struggling in a relationship at the moment, you'll gain powerful insights and tools to use when the need arises.

People (and relationships) are destroyed by lack of knowledge. After you read the stories of others stuck along the road to their emotional, relational and behavioral healing, you will come to see clearly why this happens. You'll also learn what options are available for getting unstuck.

If you are recovering from an addiction, codependency, or abuse of any kind, this book is a must. If you are an educator, this book is a great tool for conveying healthy concepts and practical examples to your students. Churches too can benefit by using the material directly from the pulpit or in small group settings.

Individuals usually don't come to me for counseling when things are going well. And I rarely hear from prospective clients who are having difficulties with their pets, automobiles or plumbing! No, people seek me out when their relationships are not working. Relationships are the most important thing in the universe, and if they are not healthy, life is difficult if not downright empty. When relationships are working as they should, however, everything seems right with the world!

Among the most important relationships are those with family. Within the family the human race not only procreates but its individuals achieve a sense of who they are. Ideally it is an environment where all feel unconditionally loved and accepted. They then take what they have learned from their family to the outside world, extending the concept of who and what they are.

Society itself depends upon our ability to initiate and sustain appropriate relationships. For instance, those in business must be able to build relationships to sell their products and services. And where would we be without the communities of law enforcement, education and health care? These institutions that are so intrinsic to our society are borne out of relationships and our compassion for one another.

When the security and trust of a relationship deteriorates, many of us instinctively employ coping mechanisms to try and fix the problem. These behaviors, which almost always prove unsuccessful, result in what I hear most in my office: Why am I staying stuck in this poor relationship? Why isn't my love enough to change my circumstances or this other person? If I continue to show love to this person, they *will* eventually step up to the plate and make life easy and tolerable for me, right? They *will* give in and see my point of view, right? Not necessarily. Just because we are nice and cooperative doesn't mean we'll get the response we want or expect. This is why many of us stay stuck. As a former pastor and now as a Licensed Clinical Pastoral Counselor

(L.C.P.C.), I investigate three areas when relationships are stuck:

- the body, which includes any chemical, physiological or biological abnormality,

- the soul, which consists of the mind, the will, and the emotions (which together make up personality), along with inborn temperament traits, and

- the spirit, which includes spiritual insight and one's belief system about God.

I look at these three components as a three-legged table. Even if only one leg is removed, the table will not stand. And the unhappy truth is, some individuals have had all three legs knocked out from under them.

I have seen many people, including faithful, church-going Christians, who continue to suffer with emotional, behavioral and relational issues even when they receive plenty of love, support and attention.

I see some attending megachurches struggling with relapsing relationships because they make one poor decision after another, even when they have received unconditional love and acceptance. While these large churches often have great marketing plans to attract the masses, they still need to find ways to resolve their members' dysfunctional entanglements. In other words, these churches do a wonderful job of fishing for men, but not so good a job of cleaning them! I have witnessed many congregations desperately implement small groups, lay counselors, weekend retreats, prayer meetings and special healing services to help members solve problems that can only be worked through by identifying deeper clinical issues.

Many church officials I've worked with have decided that the increase in divorce, unwanted pregnancies, addictions and domestic violence is due to declining morals in our day and age. I, however, believe this is an excuse used by churches unwilling to deal with the core issues afflicting their members.

In addition, I have come to the conclusion that the reason churches in the evangelical world are experiencing more of these problems is because they are accepting people into their assemblies without restrictions. In the past, people with socially embarrassing issues were excommunicated from or unwelcome within "God's house." Nowadays there is a more open approach to receiving those who have moral or behavioral problems. The trouble is that many churches, rather than treating or eliminating these behaviors, actually end up enabling them in a codependent way.

My biggest challenge as a Licensed Clinical Pastoral Counselor has been helping those I counsel develop a mindset to stop hurtful or dysfunctional people from taking advantage of them. Many of us have been conditioned to be excessively tolerant, to turn the other cheek, love our enemies, and patiently endure abusive partners and family members. This philosophy has set the stage for a pattern of "learned helplessness." This may come from faulty Biblical teachings that we perhaps grew up with, as well as from some overly sensitive "Christian" values influencing society as a whole. Personally, I do not interpret the Bible and its principles this way; neither do I see God as a codependent enabler.

Some clients come to my office expecting me to change the person they're having a problem with. Many seem to believe wishful thinking can solve their problems. This kind of "false faith" is an effort to avoid confrontation and rejection. What I help counselees understand and incorporate into their lives is the idea that, rather than focusing on changing the other person, they must risk changing themselves.

There are logical explanations for why some people don't change in spite of our love for them. Still, we're left asking ourselves: Why do we continue to argue and fight? Why do we keep finding ourselves in financial straits? Why do our children behave the way they do? Why do our spouses continue to drink? How can anyone do these things when we love them, treat them with respect, sacrifice for them — even cover up for them? Oh God, where are you, and why isn't my love enough?

It can all become a desperate quagmire from which we see no escape for ourselves or for those we care about. Why *do* we stay stuck?

Chapter 1

Anger and the Law of Unmet Expectations

Most people have a distorted image of anger. In our politically correct society, anger is a behavior that is often categorized as barbaric. An angry person is frequently portrayed as uncivilized, uneducated and even immoral! More often than not, this is hardly the case.

From childhood many of us were conditioned to believe that we shouldn't express anger — and if we do, oh boy, are we in trouble! I have observed that those who as children were not allowed to display any form of anger appear to have many depressive problems when they become adults. Could it be this is because they have more covert and displaced anger than those who as children were allowed to vent justifiable anger?

In this chapter, we'll explore where anger comes from and how to transform it from a liability into an asset.

Where Does Anger Come From?

Believe it or not, anger comes from one place only, and that is through an *unmet expectation*. Yes, that's what I said! Anger comes only from unmet expectations. It is as absolute as the law of gravity. When our expectations are not met, we become angry.

For example, imagine you are on an escalator packed with people and see a frantic mother fighting her way through the crowd as she calls to a small child just beyond you. In that scenario, you probably wouldn't be surprised if she shoved her way past you to reach her child. And you probably wouldn't be angry because you expect a mother to shove her way through to rescue her child. But if you had not seen or heard the mother coming and didn't know what she was doing, you probably would have felt an initial flash of anger. You didn't *expect* to be shoved.

Some people, especially those who are tenderhearted, passive, or were born with a meek temperament, flinch from the idea of saying they're angry. Instead, they say, "I'm not angry — I'm hurt." But saying you're hurt is often just a more polite way of saying you're angry.

In the same way, when people steal from, lie to, or betray us, our natural tendency is to get angry or hurt. We feel that way because we simply didn't *expect* to be mistreated. "How dare they shove me!" we say to ourselves. Every time a person, place or thing does not meet our expectations, we *will* experience hurt and anger.

Problems with expectations arise when we are unable to decipher between an expectation that is legitimate and one that isn't. Often I ask counselees to make a list of all their expectations. In most cases their list contains preconceived ideas that are, frankly, unrealistic. I explain that if they continue to harbor these illusions along with the discontent and bitterness the unrealistic expectations produce, they will remain in a constant state of anger. Somewhere along the way the folks who struggle with unrealistic expectations have developed the attitude that they deserve or are entitled to something that is just not possible from the average relationship — even healthy ones. They're expecting someone else to fix their discontent or lack of fulfillment.

Some parents come to me for counseling because of the constant arguing and resistance they are getting from their teenager. After a deeper look and after meeting with the teen, I often find that the parents are acting unrealistically. In many cases, the parents have projected their own fears and failures onto their child, even before the teen has done anything remotely wrong. The teen is completely unaware of the presumptions their parents have burdened them with.

I say to these parents: "What did you expect? Teenagers act like teenagers. If you expect your teen to act like an adult all of the time, you will be in a constant state of anger and disappointment."

This is not to say that parents should condone unhealthy, destructive or disruptive behavior. It does mean they should pick their battles.

In the same way, unmet expectations can become a problem with married couples.

Nick & Mary's Story

One day, a middle-aged woman I'll call "Mary" came to me for counseling because of the anger she was feeling toward her husband. She said that "Nick" had cheated on her several times in the early stages of their marriage, and she now suspected, after 19 years of marriage and two children, that he was having an affair with his secretary.

Mary was enraged. She screamed out in my office, "I'm so angry I'm going to blow! What can I do about this rage inside me?"

I then asked her a few questions: "You said Nick cheated on you several times in the past?"

"Yes," she answered.

"Why did you stay with him?" I asked. "What convinced you that he wouldn't do this again?"

Her answer was one I often get: "Nick seemed sorry, and he promised he wouldn't do it again."

"And you believed him."

"Yes," she replied.

"Well, then, what did you expect?" I asked and then went on, "If Nick treated you like this several times in the past and was never held accountable for his behavior, why should he change? You never left him. You still cooked his dinners, did his laundry, gave him sex, cleaned his home and raised his children. Nick was actually rewarded for having his cake and eating it, too."

After meeting with Mary a few more times, she realized that the change that needed to take place would have to begin with her. She understood that her husband's pattern of adultery would cause her to live in a constant state of anger and rage until she set boundaries and changed her expectations of him. She finally recognized that Nick would have to suffer personal loss and be soundly challenged with real consequences in order for him to stop his predictable M.O.

Mary soon learned to *expect* her husband to continue in this pattern until his actions caused him to hit bottom. Also, Mary needed to set and follow through with strong boundaries that would protect her and the children from Nick's behavior. Many men and women live in a revolving door of unmet expectations and anger because they do not change their circumstances. Rather than take action and make it hard for the other person to keep behaving so poorly, they sit in their mess like a frog in boiling water. They are too afraid — too afraid of what the other person's reaction will be or too afraid of losing that person altogether — to make the leap to change.

When you find that love isn't enough to remove your unresolved anger, and you feel stuck, it may well be due to unrealistic or unmet expectations.

Forced Entry:
No Boundaries, Lots of Anger

One of the most common errors couples make is this: Once they get married, they fail to set and/or ignore healthy boundaries. Even though married couples should be able to share meals and money, bodies and beds, their individuality and privacy still need to be respected. When boundaries aren't honored, expectations won't be met, and tempers may start to flare.

Mark & Amy's Story

It's not uncommon for married couples to come to me for counseling as a last-ditch effort before calling it quits. Such was the case for Mark and Amy. As I met with them, the issue became clear. When Amy wanted attention from Mark, she would become critical, delivering nasty jabs and sarcastic remarks. Apparently, these antics were meant to signal Mark that he needed to give her the time and attention she felt she deserved.

Amy expected that the man she married would not treat her the way her father had treated her mother. Amy's image of her mother was that of a gullible doormat, and she saw her father as a deadbeat. Apparently he was a passive fellow who was very apathetic toward her mother. Long before Amy married, she decided her marriage would be nothing like her parents'. She would not put up with a man who treated her anything like her father treated her mother, so whenever Mark did anything resembling her father's behavior, Amy's controlling actions would escalate. It was difficult for Mark to go golfing with his buddies or take any time for himself. And it would turn *really* ugly if he forgot to plan out every moment of the weekend to have fun and romance with Amy.

Amy had an unrealistic "chick flick" notion of marriage. When family and friends pointed out her overly idealistic presumptions about married life, Amy would not concede. Every time Mark did not live up to what she considered were his relational duties, Amy would try to manipulate him into feeling guilty about being a bad husband.

As Amy's tenacious behavior persisted, Mark would run out of energy and patience. This pushed Mark to revert to his instinctual coping skills — which in his case meant leaving to find a place of peace and solitude. Amy would then shift into high gear, going to the place where Mark had sought refuge. She would grab him, yell, and demand he come home. She would tell Mark he had no right to walk away from her, especially when they were in the middle of an argument.

Amy became so desperate that she determined to keep Mark from leaving their home — at all. She would block the door and hide the keys to his car. Amy's need to make him conform to the husbandly image in her mind was so strong that she would scream and throw a fit until he gave in. She was actually violating Mark's ability to decide whether he wanted to be with her or not.

This is the type of aggressive boundary that says, "I can choose to be with you or not, regardless of how you might feel about the issue." This boundary is one that even God does not violate. You see, Amy couldn't *afford* to have her expectations not met. Her need to live up to her idealized standards would not allow her to retreat, swallow her pride, or settle for what she considered was traditional and boring. While Amy had the right to choose to stay married to Mark, she did not have the right to force him to conform to her will.

After Mark set the boundary with Amy that he didn't want to be married to her anymore unless drastic changes were made, Amy began to listen. She learned it was not acceptable to force entry into another person's life, even if it is her husband's. Amy also learned that when she allowed Mark to choose to meet her expectations, or to choose not to meet them, he was much more willing to cooperate with her.

Amy found that talking lovingly to Mark and gently asking questions, instead of being demanding and forceful, was more effective in building her relationship with him. She also learned that if Mark chose not to live the way she wanted him to, and even chose not to love or stay married to her at all, she would have to accept that fact. Amy found that she shouldn't expect anyone to love, conform, or commit to her if they choose not to. She learned that she could only set boundaries for herself, and that she could remove only her own fears and unrealistic expectations, not anyone else's. Eventually, Amy did come to realize that Mark wasn't like her father, and that he had no intention of treating Amy as her dad had treated her mother.

There are only two things a person can do with expectations: adjust them or do away with them altogether. Amy's unrealistic expectations needed to be removed. When they were, her anger naturally went away. We must consider that lack of boundaries and forced entry into another's life may keep us stuck in an angry relationship.

When a need becomes a demand, it is called abuse.

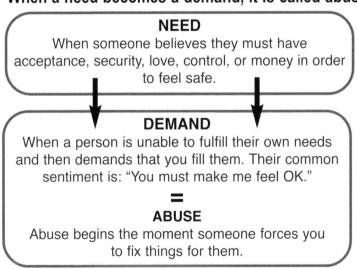

NEED
When someone believes they must have acceptance, security, love, control, or money in order to feel safe.

DEMAND
When a person is unable to fulfill their own needs and then demands that you fill them. Their common sentiment is: "You must make me feel OK."

=

ABUSE
Abuse begins the moment someone forces you to fix things for them.

Chapter 2

Hidden Sources of Anger

Several types of unresolved anger produce the uncontrollable rages we see in some people's lives. When people stay stuck in conflicts that involve anger toward themselves or others, there is a reason lurking beneath the surface.

In my practice, the three forms of hidden anger I see most often are: displaced anger, passive-aggressive anger, and fear-based anger.

Displaced Anger
and
Jim's Story

Forty-year-old Jim came to me for counseling after he had been served divorce papers. Jim provided well for his family. Friends at church referred to him as a pillar of the congregation, and many revered him. But while others saw Jim as a polite, even-tempered person, he actually harbored a deep anger. That anger was toward his wife of 18 years, and it was out of control.

Jim admitted his wife could no longer take his anger. I asked him if he had ever physically hurt his wife. His bottom lip began to quiver; then, through tears he confessed that during fits of rage he had slapped, pushed and shoved his wife. Because she loved him so much and was afraid of what might happen to their family, she had never called the police. Many men and women live like Jim. They have uncontrollable anger, which they direct toward the person they love most. It seems like the closer their spouse gets to them, the angrier they become.

When individuals come to me for counseling, I ask them to fill out an evaluation form that asks a variety of questions about their family of origin. It includes questions about their parents, siblings, divorce, abuse, etc. After looking at their answers, I am usually able to assess the problem.

From Jim's questionnaire it was apparent that his father was very critical of him. As Jim and I talked, he shared that when he was young his father would punish him for getting a bad grade, spilling his drink, or other minor infractions. Jim was never able to satisfy his dad, regardless of what he accomplished. Unfortunately, Jim's mother was a very passive woman who feared confronting her husband about the way he treated Jim and his brothers. Jim also shared with me that his two brothers "went wild" once they left for college and eventually dropped out of school. One became an alcoholic. Each brother's reaction to the abuse was manifested in one unhealthy form or another.

As I listened to Jim's story, I realized that he was a victim of displaced anger — and therefore a prime example of the saying that goes, "Hurt people hurt people." Jim victimized his wife because he himself had been victimized. Because Jim felt helpless against his father's abuse, he misdirected the anger he felt for his father toward his wife. He began to mimic his father's behavior.

An illustration I share with those who are suffering from someone's displaced anger is the train wreck effect. Have you ever heard a freight train come to a stop? Crash! Slam! Screech! Boom! It's the same with "railroad cars" of anger and hurt. Incident after incident fills the cars until something ignites memory cells in the brain, triggering all those cars to slam into each other. The person standing in the path of this locomotive will feel the full impact of all the accumulated hurt and anger. This is called "rage."

Jim's wife couldn't take the abuse any longer. She thought Jim was a mean, hateful person who simply had a bad attitude, especially toward her. She felt he couldn't possibly love her if he treated her this way and that it had been a horrible mistake to marry him.

It's understandable that she would feel that way. On the other hand, Jim himself didn't comprehend why he treated her as he did. Once Jim understood what displaced anger was and received counseling and instruction on how to remove pains from the past, he slowly began to restore his relationship with his wife. I also helped Jim learn how to confront those who had directly hurt him in the past, instead of displacing his anger toward his family.

Many people are walking time bombs because of what happened to them in the past, either long ago or only minutes before. Because they are unable, unwilling or unaware of how to properly resolve the conflict, they are left with displaced anger. It's the kind of rage that can result in school shootings, workplace massacres, domestic violence, road rage, and child abuse. Displaced anger is destructive to individuals, to families and to society as a whole. Learning to recognize it can help us know when to seek professional help and move forward in life.

Passive-Aggressive Anger
and
George and Sally's Story

Sally was a 42-year-old housewife who came to me because of her strained marriage. She was troubled by the fact that her husband, George, appeared to have so little interest in her. She told me that they had been married only a few years when he began to shut down whenever she shared her feelings or wanted affection:

> He told me he felt like I was nagging or controlling him, so there was nothing more to talk about. The more he shut down, the more aggressively I pursued an answer or reaction from him. Now my family and friends have pegged me as the crazy one. It seems like I'm the one who is angry and out of control,

and he seems to be the one who is calm and in control. Now, 15 years later, George lives in his part of the house and I live in mine. I am so angry. I can't get him to do what I want him to. We just exist in the same house like two roommates.

Sally was like many who come to me for counseling, thinking I should call the "disobedient" spouse on the phone and read them the riot act until they agree to comply. I am sure that if I had made George feel guilty about his behavior, it would have eliminated much of Sally's anger. However, even when I have the opportunity to do that to one spouse, I don't, because it does not resolve the couple's root conflict. What I prefer to do is encourage each spouse to share with me his or her perspective on the dispute. From this point I can identify the real issue and help each partner learn how to be responsible for his or her own actions.

In this particular case, George finally did come in to see me. He was a quiet and polite man. After meeting with him for about 20 minutes, he almost had me convinced how out of control Sally was and how innocent and in control he was. He said that after their first child was born, his wife had changed completely.

"Everything we used to do together just stopped," he said. "She didn't like me drinking anymore. Before we had children, Sally would drink with me. She made me throw out some of the adult movies we used to watch together, and she started demanding that we connect on an emotional level, which makes me uncomfortable."

George went on in the same vein for some time. Finally, after his long discourse, I asked, "What did you do to try to ease some of Sally's fears as a new mother? What did you expect from a woman who just had a baby?"

George squirmed. "I am a good person," he said. "I provide well for Sally and the kids. What else does she want from me? Why did she become a saint all of a sudden? She tricked me. Besides, I never really wanted kids."

Then it happened, as it so often does in my office. When I pushed his buttons, the George who appeared to be the innocent party, the one who seemed so controlled and victimized, finally blew. The anger and negativity he tried so hard to conceal was exposed.

As George revealed his true colors, I concluded that he was passive-aggressively punishing his wife by creating an environment that made her look insane. He wanted to get back at her for defying what he thought was normal. George punished Sally by ignoring her, moving out of the bedroom, and deliberately not cooperating with her concerning their children.

This passive-aggressive behavior succeeded in making George look good to friends and family. Passive-aggressive anger is a slow, painful death for the one upon whom it is inflicted. It causes its victims to think they're going crazy, especially if they are committed to doing everything they can to preserve the relationship. In this case, Sally continued to try to fix the marriage George was maliciously sabotaging. It was a covert display of anger that allowed George to look like the good guy.

Children too can learn passive-aggressive behavior. Some quickly figure out how to manipulate their parents by getting into trouble at school, stealing money out of dresser drawers, or engaging in promiscuous activity. When I worked in adolescent treatment centers, I saw many teenagers act out by self-mutilating in order to make their parents suffer.

Passive aggressors should be held responsible for their actions. The best way to combat passive-aggressive anger is to refuse to be manipulated. We should not fear what might happen if they continue to pull away from us. If they threaten to leave or stop loving us just because we're making positive changes in the relationship, we must remember they would have left anyway.

Unfortunately, many of us will stay stuck in a passive-aggressive cycle until we learn to identify and defeat it. A good way to do that is to stand our ground and confront the offenders, rather than either attacking or conforming to their manipulations.

Fear & Anger
and
The Puppy Lesson

While a college student I heard that a family was giving away Labrador/German shepherd puppies. In retrospect, I can't figure out why I would have wanted a dog while attending college, but I did. I went to the farm where the family lived, and there, out by the barn, were the puppies: fluffy, black and gold fur balls with eyes peeking out. Their clumsy paws looked too big for their little round bodies. As they climbed over one another whimpering and biting, I saw the biggest of the litter huddled in the corner, clearly afraid of all the commotion. I told the owners, "I want that one. Yes, the one over there in the corner."

Silly me. I thought that I would give a big, timid pup a good, secure home and then he wouldn't feel so afraid. But after a few months, I was disappointed. It seemed the puppy was never going to shake off his timidity. Whenever anyone tried to pick him up, he would squeal, urinate on the floor, and stick his tail between his legs. He was the ultimate sissy dog!

Then, about the time he reached "doggy adolescence" and the testosterone kicked in, I noticed a change. Rather than being fearful when strangers approached, he would snarl, growl and sometimes even snap. Where he once acted cowardly, he now attacked aggressively. Even though he was very loving and loyal to family members, he was mean toward anything or anyone else. He chased all animals and people from the property. No one was able to enter his domain without someone in the family going out to reassure him that everything was OK. He became the ultimate macho watchdog.

I soon consulted a veterinarian, explaining to him about Rover's recent unwelcome transformation. A knowing smile grew on the doctor's face. If I was looking for a junkyard dog, he said, then I picked the right puppy. The more fearful a dog is as a puppy, the angrier it becomes as an adult, the vet said. He went on to explain that because of Rover's inborn fear, he had created an innate defense mechanism to protect himself. He became ferocious in order to ward off anything that might hurt him. In other words, he was going to attack *it* before it attacked *him*! His fear had turned into anger and aggressiveness.

Wow! A light turned on, and I started to understand why some people are so angry and live their lives barking, biting and attacking others. I saw the origin of my own aggressive nature. It's because we are afraid. As children we may have been scared and timid, but at some point we were hurt so badly that we developed a defense mechanism to protect ourselves from ever being hurt again.

It's very important to understand that most angry people are filled with fears. Fearful people always expect to be hurt, so they jump the gun. They hurt you before you hurt them. But if we can mend the fear, the anger will dissipate. This kind of fear is another reason some people stay stuck en route to their relational healing.

Chapter 3

What About Forgiveness?

When people set healthy boundaries and don't allow others to destroy, abuse, or dictate their lives, they are very often accused of being unforgiving and uncaring.

Aren't we *supposed* to forgive? you may ask. Aren't most people angry, depressed and bitter because they refuse to forgive? Don't we *have* to forgive in order to be forgiven by God, others, and even ourselves?

Although that's the way some preachers, counselors, psychotherapists and self-help authors teach it, I believe that particular notion of forgiveness is misguided, to say the least. It further victimizes and delays victims' healing to insist that they must forgive everyone for everything. That kind of arbitrary absolution is what I call false forgiveness.

My question has always been: How can you forgive people who have hurt, maimed, degraded, betrayed and abused you unless they have completely changed in their behavior toward you and, furthermore, have *asked* for your forgiveness? I believe a victim should never forgive a perpetrator unless the offender is willing to accept fault and has completely made things right.

Those who consider themselves unforgiving people usually think of themselves this way because they are still angry toward someone who has hurt them. Well, they *should* feel anger toward their abuser. Sometimes anger toward the person who has wronged them is healthy. It moves victims out of feeling helpless.

There can be a problem with this type of anger, though. It can keep us from detaching ourselves from the one hurting us. Instead, we stay angry because we can't get our abuser to say they're sorry for what they've done. When the people who have rejected us and turned our life upside down act as if they're enjoying life while we suffer, it isn't fair. We want them to feel the loss, sorrow and hurt that we've felt. But we also want them to love us again. We want them to accept us again. So, we think that by arbitrarily forgiving them the pain will go away and we will be freed from any resentment and bitterness, when what we really need to do is just let them go.

I've had clients who felt they had to forgive someone because their family, friends and minister kept telling them it was wrong of them not to. Most people who impose such a guilt trip on victims have an ulterior motive. They may want the abuser's infractions to remain hidden, they may be impatient with the victim's pain, or they may themselves dread the abuser's anger. Why should victims compromise their expectations for reconciliation, especially if the perpetrator will not change or admit any wrongdoing? It is the *perpetrator's* responsibility to right the wrong and ask the victim for forgiveness. And if that hasn't happened, then the victim would do better to focus his or her energy on letting go rather than forgiving someone who has neither asked for nor earned it.

The forgiveness process — and it *is* a process — implies reconciliation and the rebuilding of the relationship. But to "let go" means "I am okay, regardless." Letting go means accepting that the other person is gone, never to return. Letting go also means accepting the perpetrator's refusal to admit that they have wronged you. Letting go means coming to terms with the fact that, even though we may not see justice done at the moment, we nevertheless are making a conscious decision to not let it rule our lives in a negative, bitter manner. Falsely forgiving a perpetrator will not fix our anger, but letting go will.

Many people go to the Bible looking for the answer to what true forgiveness is. What they find is that God doesn't forgive us in order to fix His own anger or to benefit Himself in any way. The God of the Holy Bible does, however, require repentance before He forgives. The Bible also mentions that we ought to forgive others even as God has forgiven us. That means we too should require repentance — or in other words, a turnaround in behavior. In Chapter 17 of the Gospel of Luke, Jesus tells his disciples that if a brother sins against you, "rebuke him," but if he repents (turns around), forgive him. It's funny that many Christians who read this passage somehow seem to skim over the "rebuke" part. They also disregard the "if he repents" part.

Forgiveness is not necessarily meant to heal the one who is doing the forgiving; it is meant to heal or reconcile the *relationship*. Although true forgiveness does bring healing and its benefits to all parties involved, the precedent God established for forgiveness is one designed to benefit the relationship as a whole.

It may just be a matter of semantics, but because of the confusion and accompanying guilt and shame about what it means to forgive and to let go, I feel it is extremely important to understand and explain the distinct differences. Ideally, we pursue "letting go" when it comes to the chronically abusive people in our lives. Forgiveness, on the other hand, is something we want to receive and extend when change is evident within the other person. We benefit when we learn to decipher and live within the realistic expectations of either letting go or forgiving.

Now, if you have been the person who has wronged another, or your behavior has created an unnecessary distance or separation with someone, then you don't need to forgive — you need to *ask for* forgiveness. You also need to make right whatever wrong you inflicted upon the other person. If you complete these steps and the other person then refuses to forgive you, then that person truly becomes the unforgiving person. The burden lies with them.

For both parties, the act of forgiving oftentimes causes more pain because each will have to change or "make an about-face" with their behavior. This takes work and commitment.

The only time I believe you should forgive people who haven't asked for forgiveness and/or changed their behavior toward you is when they didn't understand what they were doing. As Jesus said: "Forgive them, for they know not what they are doing." Then you might find relief in understanding that someone's pure ignorance played a major role in the offense.

Just suppose, for example, that you have a grandmother who punished you several times too harshly but thought she was doing the right thing, at least according to her old-fashioned convictions. Then she dies before you have the chance to confront her about the spankings that so hurt your feelings. I would think that you could find it in your heart to forgive Grandma, at least once you came to the conclusion that she didn't spank you because she wanted to hurt you but because she honestly thought she was helping. Although Grandma might not be alive for you to know the full truth, you could conclude her innocence based on what you know about her. In other words, those whose intentions are well-meaning are more likely to be sorry and repent if only they could understand their transgression. On that basis, it makes sense to go ahead and forgive them.

However, there are many situations where spouses, ex-lovers, con artists, rapists, robbers, murderers, pedophiles, etc. know exactly what they have done and are doing to their victims. These offenders need not be forgiven by you or anyone else. The burden lies on them to change and make restitution.

Furthermore, it is very important to learn how to forgive yourself by following the same criteria you expect from anyone else. You may need to ask yourself for forgiveness and then let go of the "demons" that have been tormenting you. In this way you can become both the initiator and recipient of true forgiveness.

In conclusion, to say you have forgiven those who have knowingly offended you without your confronting them or without their asking to be forgiven does not bring about true forgiveness. You may only be excusing their behavior, which may make you feel relief for the moment until the pain resurfaces.

For long-term healing and true forgiveness that will reconcile the relationship, there must be repentance from the offender, or willingness from you to let go of them to not stay stuck in the "false forgiveness" trap.

Because some refuse or feel they are unable to let go of hurt and anger, they become engulfed with feelings of regret and bitterness. But those who don't want to stay stuck in a trap of self-pity do so by following these top 10 ways to break free:

Top 10 Ways to Overcome
Regret and Bitterness

1. View mistakes as a learning experience, not as a loss.

2. Stop focusing on what others have done to you and examine instead what you have allowed them to do to you. Take responsibility and set appropriate boundaries.

3. Stay busy achieving and progressing, and do not focus on the past.

4. Focus on what you *can* have, not on what you once had.

5. Detach from individuals, organizations and belief systems that keep you tied to regrets. This can be a church, job or club. This may also mean eliminating some family gatherings as well as time spent with former in-laws or old friends.

6. Let go of those people who haven't qualified for your forgiveness because they haven't repented or made restitution toward you.

7. Grieve for and accept past losses, including friendships, family, inheritances, money, and other material things.

8. Invest in counseling, seminars and support groups that can educate and encourage you to remove blocks and dispel fears from the past.

9. Remove superstitions and false beliefs because they produce uncertainty. Examples are: fearing God's punishment if you set boundaries with others, fear of being left destitute and penniless, fear of being alone, etc.

10. Find people with whom you can safely share your experiences and feelings.

Chapter 4
Circumstantial Depression

Sometimes those who have wronged us accept that they have done so and change their life and behaviors. At other times they are punished for their wrongs, receiving some well-deserved justice. When either of these happens, our anger dissipates into the expanse of the universe, never to be seen again!

But what happens when we are wronged and there are no clear changes or consequences? When it comes to seeing that someone pays for what they've done to us, we are often rendered helpless. Such unresolved feelings of powerlessness often happen following divorce, abuse, and crimes such as rape. So what happens when the closure we crave never materializes? Where does the anger go? Do we retaliate, withdraw, fight, or simply do nothing?

Anger has an uncanny ability to disguise itself and worm its way out in other forms. One of the hidden forms of unresolved anger is depression. Depression is a direct result of prolonged anger. The top 10 signs of depression I see most often in my counseling practice are:

- withdrawal

- excessive sleeping

- insomnia

- irritability and negativity

- angry outbursts

- lack of ambition

- critical of self and others

- trivial business (constantly busy with unnecessary tasks)

- excessive and irresponsible spending, and

- alcohol and drug abuse. (Many depressed people self-medicate with legal and illegal drugs and alcohol.)

Unresolved anger turns into bitterness, and bitterness turns into resentment. And when anger, bitterness and resentment continue to compound, they manifest as depression. Once again, anger turned inward (feeling powerless) becomes depression. This is why many homicidal people end up committing suicide.

Anger is directly related to depression. Just as it is impossible for people to get hurt and angry other than

48

through an unmet expectation, it is also impossible to get circumstantially depressed except through anger turned inward. Anger imprisoned inside always leads to depression. You see, unresolved anger never just goes away. It is like energy: it can be neither created nor destroyed; it can only be transferred. It shows itself as addictions, bad habits, and unrestrained behavior.

Many depressed people have lost track of *why* or *when* they became resentful, bitter and angry. It may have been eons ago. But once a person shows signs of depression, a skilled counselor should be able to trace the anger back to its origin — in other words, that period of time when the person was unable to resolve their anger. Counselors probing the past of someone who is depressed inevitably find hurt, abuse, rejection and pain. They also find many unmet expectations.

Countless people live with regret and depression because as children they couldn't take an active role in resolving their anger. Childhood should be a period of innocence when young ones are able to trust the adults in their lives, but children held captive by dysfunctional adults are often incapable of deciphering between right and wrong when they grow up.

It's my conclusion that this "adult supervision disorder" gives way to negligence, makes children vulnerable for abuse, and causes many devastating and long-term effects. It can cause the next generation to hurt, destroy, self-medicate or drop out of life. If we were able to educate adults to be nurturing, unselfish and wise parents, most societal problems would disappear. But when children live with abusive parents or caretakers they cannot fight back against, they're likely to become angry, depressed adults. And thus the cycle goes on. The feelings that resulted from their childhood helplessness must heal in order for them to truly recover from circumstantial depression later on.

Depression is quickly becoming the number one reason people seek medical attention and counseling; meanwhile, it destroys families, friends and finances. When anger about things in the past isn't properly dealt with, its victims can lose years of their life that could have been fun, financially prosperous, and full of cherished memories.

Aunt Sophie

I remember Aunt Sophie coming to my childhood home to help clean, do laundry, and take care of me and my 10 brothers and sisters. (With such a large family, my parents needed all the help they could get!) Often, as Aunt Sophie dusted off family pictures, she would start talking loudly to herself, then break out in a frightful sob. She would carry on about how good she had it before her alcoholic husband destroyed their marriage. She would mumble and lament aloud as if it had all happened only yesterday, when in reality it had happened years before. She never remarried, her son disowned her, and we dreaded being around her. Sadly, at the age of 84, Aunt Sophie died alone and defeated.

As I became a student of human behavior, it became obvious to me that Aunt Sophie had not healed from what is known as "learned helplessness." She was always sad and depressed because she felt she couldn't go on after her abusive marriage ended. This tendency must have been present in our family genes, because my dad (Sophie's brother) did the same thing. His learned helplessness was manifested, not as typical depression, but as rage. Both Aunt Sophie's sorrowful sobbing and my father's angry outbursts came from the same source. For years, I would watch my father go into a tirade about family and friends who supposedly had betrayed him years before.

When I heard him yelling about people and incidents I knew nothing about, I would ask my mother, "Who are those people Dad is complaining about?"

In her meek voice she would answer, "They were just folks he knew twenty years ago, but they're dead now."

My dad carried on this way until he died an early death due to congestive heart failure at age 57. In those days, the medical profession didn't know what they do today about circumstantial depression. If it isn't detected and dealt with, circumstantial depression will keep a relationship and a family stuck in misery.

Clinical Depression

Even though depression can be caused by life's circumstances, it also can be caused by a chemical or hormonal imbalance in the brain or regulatory system. This is called clinical depression. If one of the glands that regulates our body goes haywire, our physical chemistry can be thrown off enough to make us feel awful. Sometimes when one chemical or hormone is out of balance, it causes a disruptive domino effect throughout our entire body.

The result is that it becomes difficult to accomplish even the smallest tasks. Our energy level and ambition are either squelched or heightened, based on whether there is a deficiency or surplus of the testosterone, estrogen, adrenaline, serotonin, etc. in our system.

When our physical chemistry makes us unable to perform to our potential, we experience unmet expectations. Unmet expectations then make us angry. And if we can't figure out what is making us frustrated and angry, we become depressed. This is the pattern.

Much like circumstantial depression, clinical depression comes from inwardly turned anger, an anger borne of unmet expectations. The difference is that the root of clinical depression is a chemical imbalance. The solution, of course, is to correct the chemical imbalance or glandular dysfunction that is causing the fatigue, illness or emotional darkness.

Many people live frustrated, miserable lives because they don't know they have a chemical imbalance. Marriages may suffer terribly for years because no one knows that a particularly angry spouse actually has a thyroid problem, a non-functioning pituitary or a mineral deficiency. I have seen marriages end in divorce during a woman's menopause, a stage when hormone production can be erratic. Men who experience midlife crises may be going through their own menopause, with hormonal changes causing unpredictable behavior.

Some individuals simply need better nutrition or medical care to help mend these deficiencies. For the last two years, my wife and I have been treated by a chiropractor trained in a therapeutic process called the Pettibon system. These treatments to our necks and backs have greatly improved the nerve supply to the areas that control hormones and behavior.

My wife has seen drastic improvement in her menopausal mood swings and says, "It feels like a dark cloud lifts off me when the doctor adjusts my neck." All communication from the brain to the rest of the body must pass through the cervical vertebrae in the neck. If that passageway is slightly misaligned or impeded, the blockage acts like a dimmer switch to the rest of your body, and the glands and organs below your neck can suffer, even if you do not have neck pain. If your behavior and emotions are suffering, it might be wise to find a chiropractor who uses a Pettibon treatment style.

Some couples blame one another for the cyclical patterns of arguments and addictions that have left their relationship empty and hopeless. They lose years believing their spouse has a bad attitude, communication issues, a spending problem, or an addiction, when the reality is that their loved one suffers from a chemical imbalance that has made them clinically depressed.

Scott and Cindy's Story

One young couple came to me for counseling because they were fighting quite often. When I say fights, I mean literal physical altercations. Cindy was so angry and depressed that even the most trivial of requests from Scott would set her off, and she would shove and hit him. Scott and Cindy also had a 2-year-old daughter, and I was very concerned for her.

I told Cindy that either she or Scott would end up jailed on domestic violence charges with thousands of dollars in legal fees unless they corrected their problem.

As Cindy laid out her complaints against Scott, I found her expectations of him to be unrealistic and unfounded. The *real* problem for Cindy was that she was tired. As the day wore on and her energy waned, so did her tolerance, and both were completely depleted by the time her husband got home from work. She then expected him to clean house, care for their daughter, and make her feel better about herself, all at the same time. Scott did try to do most of what she expected, but to no avail. Cindy still was not happy.

I asked Cindy to come back alone for counseling. Meeting with her one-on-one was important in this case because of the heightened emotions and negative tension between her and her husband. When I met with Cindy, I asked about her family history and learned that many of her relatives, including her father, aunts, uncles, brothers and sisters, suffered from depression, alcoholism and paranoia, even to the point that some had committed suicide.

Even though Cindy and Scott had been to counseling before, Cindy had always given the appearance of stability and confidence, so their previous counselors only treated the obvious symptoms, with little success. They told the couple to communicate with each other (whatever that means), hold hands and be nice to one another (whatever that means), and to take breaks from each other (whatever that means), but they apparently never entertained the notion that Cindy could be clinically depressed.

After hearing her horrific family history, I urged Scott to take Cindy to see a doctor, preferably a neuropsychiatrist, and get an evaluation. There was no doubt in my mind that Cindy had a genetic predisposition for clinical depression.

Like many, Scott was skeptical of medications used for behavioral problems and believed that individuals should simply "straighten up their attitudes." He thought taking psychotropic medications was a sign of weakness. It didn't help that others in his church told Scott that taking such medications showed a lack of faith and were "from the devil."

All this made it difficult for me to convince Scott that Cindy needed to get checked for depression. But when I was able to show him such beliefs were neither scriptural nor realistic, he finally consented.

About two weeks later, I received a call from a very elated Scott. "Mr. Joseph, I took my wife to the doctor as you recommended, and he prescribed an antidepressant," he said. "Cindy is another person! I never believed that she would ever feel good, or act happy toward me or our daughter again. Thank you, thank you, for helping."

Scott and Cindy's experience bears out another important point: Always check with a medical doctor if you see signs of clinical depression in you or your relationships. This could be one reason you are staying stuck.

Chapter 5

Bipolar Mood Disorder

L et's begin this chapter by learning about something else that can keep us stuck. It's the signs for bipolar disorder as presented by Dr. Jay Carter, Psy.D., and as outlined in the Diagnostic and Statistical Manual of Mental Disorders (DSM), a handbook published by the American Psychiatric Association. The signs include:

• oversized ego

• needing, and getting, little sleep

• very talkative

• racing thoughts

• easily distracted

• hyper-focused or goal-oriented, and

• high-risk behavior (promiscuity, unprotected sex, overspending, drug use, etc.).

A person must have at least three of these seven symptoms on a consistent basis to be considered bipolar. (Remember, always consult a mental health expert for an accurate diagnosis.)

Joe and Sara's Story

Joe and Sara first met in the spring of 1976 in a small farming town in Ohio. Joe was a senior in high school and an All-American wrestler when he met his sister's friend Sara, a tall, blonde freshman. The two went out, and they continued to date after Joe went away to college. It was a rocky courtship, but the two got engaged. Then, a month before their wedding, Sara was brutally raped.

While Joe understood that her assault would require recovery, he was unaware of the many other issues at work in Sara's troubled life. Sara had come from a very dysfunctional home. Her mother was diagnosed with severe bipolar disorder and had attempted suicide several times. Her father was killed in a tragic industrial accident when Sara was only 8, which, as expected, was devastating for the young girl. The insurance money that should have been a blessing to the family instead became a curse, as Sara's mother would use it to buy airline tickets to cities all over the United States — and then have no idea how she got there. She also gave away large amounts of money to boyfriends, relatives and strangers. Before long, she had squandered the entire death benefit.

Joe had no idea that the illness with which Sara's mother suffered was highly genetic and that, even without the assault Sara had suffered, the two of them were already at risk for the same type of difficult experiences. Sure enough, not long after they were married, Sara began suffering fits of rage during which she punched holes in the wall and even leaped from moving vehicles. She would bite, punch, kick and spit whenever they had a disagreement. Sara would awake during the night screaming with nightmares and terrors. Bizarrely, she also sometimes ran off on weekends, only to find she didn't know what city she was in or how she got there. Just like Mom.

One day while Joe was at work, he received a call from a security guard telling him that his car was going to be towed if he didn't come and pick it up. Perplexed, Joe asked, "What car, and where?"

The security guard said, "Your wife said to call this number after she left on the bus to Phoenix, and that you would come and get the car."

Still confused, Joe asked, "What bus, and where?"

"Listen, sir," the guard said. "Come and get this car in one hour, or it will be towed from the Greyhound Bus Depot."

Furious with Sara, Joe found a friend to take him to pick up the car. He then drove until he caught up with the bus and his wife. He finally was able to convince her to calm down and return home. The money Sara spent during such episodes would always set the couple back financially.

Joe assumed, not surprisingly, that Sara's erratic behavior was the result of all the trauma she had experienced and that if he were patient enough — even to the point of allowing her to physically, mentally and emotionally abuse him — she eventually would be healed of her anger and the past.

But the episodes didn't stop; as a matter of fact, they became more frequent and intense. Nothing Joe did, or didn't do, could calm her untamed outbursts.

Nevertheless, after 20 years of marriage and rearing a 14-year-old son, Joe decided he could make the situation better if he and Sara had a business together. He had helped Sara write a book about her rape and abuse, and he decided they should tour the country promoting the book, which would help her heal while giving them a common goal. Sara too thought it was a good idea.

So Joe sold their home, paid off the thousands of dollars in debt Sara had accrued, pulled their son out of middle school, and moved from Colorado to South Carolina.

But after making the move, Sara started acting up all over again — punching, cursing, running away, and spending money. Joe finally realized that Sara's destructive behavior resulted from not only her childhood abuse but also from the bipolar tendencies she inherited. He finally saw that Sara was filled with a hate and rage that no one could subdue.

Joe packed his things and moved himself and his son back to Colorado. The letter he left for Sara explained that if she wanted to restore their marriage, she would have to get some medical and psychological help.

Unfortunately, she did not. Instead, Sara filed for divorce and signed full custody of their son over to Joe. She also withdrew all their money from the bank, had the car that was in Joe's name impounded, sold all their possessions, and again ran up thousands of dollars in debt.

Just one month after the divorce was final, and after the manic episode of her bipolar high had evaporated, she tried to come back into Joe's life. It was because of her extreme mood swings that she was able to instigate a nasty divorce from Joe and cause him irreparable financial damage, yet come back to him a few months later as if nothing had happened. Joe told Sara that their relationship could not be restored because of her unwillingness to get medical help and her refusal to make restitution for the extensive damage she had inflicted upon him and his family.

Sadly, Sara currently is following in her mother's footsteps. She's gone through several more relationships, destroying more folks' good names and wrecking their finances along the way. She's been arrested twice. She is without a career, family and friends, and yet she still will not get medical help for her illness.

Bipolar (once known as manic depression) is a proven mental disorder that the medical community believes is a mineral deficiency in the brain that causes individuals to swing from a manic "high" into severe depression. Those who have the severest form of bipolar disorder have a very high rate of suicide during the depressed swing. Those in the manic (the "high" or euphoric) stage can be violent, sexually promiscuous, unreasonable, high achieving, and prone to spending enormous amounts of money on senseless things. Bipolar disorder is highly genetic. Even though this condition can be treated with medication, it is common for those diagnosed with it to stop taking their medication when they start feeling better. People with bipolar disorder appear to have other symptoms that resemble narcissistic, violent and deceptive behaviors. It is questionable as to what degree the erratic behavior is caused by a chemical depletion and what is simply willful or rebellious behavior. According to Dr. Carter, a large percentage of inmates who are incarcerated for illegal drug use are diagnosed with bipolar disorder. He also goes on to state in his book, *Bipolar: The Elements of Bipolar Disorder*, that many of these drug users are self-medicating. (See Chapter 11 on self-medicating.)

Long before we understood as much as we do now about this complex mood disorder, some thought that mom, dad, grandpa, or grandma were just "mean drunks" who hated life and everyone around them. Because of the advances made in psychiatric and medical research, most individuals who suffer from substance abuse and repeated criminal activity are now examined for bipolar disorder.

When you live with a person who exhibits the behaviors of this disorder, it becomes very difficult to decipher what is, or isn't, biological. I have come to the conclusion that anyone involved with a person who is bipolar will have a difficult time coping with this bifurcated insanity, regardless of the disorder's origin. I've never known anyone with this disorder to stabilize on their own unless they were diagnosed at an early age (adolescence or before) and medication was prescribed and taken consistently.

When patients in a relationship with someone who has been diagnosed as bipolar come to see me, I instruct them to make a list of what they would need from the other person in order to restore the relationship. It is extremely important to make a very specific list of expectations. Why? Because it is so easy for emotions to override common sense.

The biggest mistake a spouse with a depressed mate can make is to receive him or her back into the relationship before demanding accountability. Because of the heightened emotions they can display while in the depressed state, bipolar individuals can be very convincing. Their loved ones, hoping for the best, often prematurely accept them back into the relationship, only to find that they eventually cycle back to an even worse state than they were before.

This is why a list must be made — and strictly adhered to. People with destructive personalities who are serious about restoration will earn their way back by making amends and repairing what they have destroyed. It is extremely important that these individuals are held accountable to this strict standard because, as they begin to feel better, they are likely to stop taking their medication and swing back to their former behavior.

Dr. Carter also makes the point that the manic state occurs when the prefrontal lobe of the bipolar brain is not functioning correctly. The prefrontal lobe is that part of the brain that anticipates possible consequences and pitfalls. Some studies indicate that this part of the brain doesn't fully develop (especially in males) until the ages of 25 to 28. This is why teens are risk takers who often do not consider the long-term outcome of their immediate actions. For the bipolar person, it means that while in a manic state their brain isn't producing the chemicals that would tell them consequences are lurking. Because their prefrontal reasoning just went out the window, they lack the ability to judge their actions as risky or "crazy." They may make investments with money they don't have, buy expensive cars on credit, and engage in extramarital affairs, honestly believing their behavior is perfectly OK.

After their loved ones find them out, manic people often are frustrated and shocked to find others so angry with them. That is when they themselves become angry and sometimes violent. Remember the law of unmet expectations? They become angry because they didn't expect their loved ones to be so incensed that they did something their prefrontal lobe had deemed perfectly normal. Those who don't become outright angry may act as if nothing has happened, as was the case with Sara.

The individual's manic state wears off when at some point their brain runs out of "happy juice," better known as serotonin, a neurotransmitter that regulates mood. At this point, the bipolar person sinks into a depression that is almost impossible to escape. They exhibit sorrow and remorse and can become quite weepy and needy. Some with bipolar disorder commit suicide during this time. The cycle continues until the sufferer finds help and is treated with medication.

It can be easy to think of individuals with this disorder as merely very charismatic and ambitious. They can seem like high achievers who simply run down after working too hard or after staying up all night planning great things! The way you can tell the difference between an ambitious person and one with bipolar disorder is the fruit of their labor and behavior, as well as the previously mentioned criteria set by the Diagnostic and Statistical Manual of Mental Disorders.

If you are dealing with someone who has bipolar disorder, you will stay stuck in your relationship with them unless you become aware of the symptoms and are willing to seek proper counseling and treatment.

Chapter 6

Low Self-Esteem and Shame

When we think of someone with low self-esteem, we may picture a depressed, lonely person who lacks confidence. Most people in our society believe we should build up such a person through positive, uplifting encouragement. I, however, do not believe that pampering can build anyone's self-esteem.

This is one example of how we have chased symptoms instead of dealing with the root cause. For example, the medical community once believed that ulcers were caused by stress. They continued to treat the overproduction of stomach acid as a band-aid approach. For years, doctors would cut out parts of the stomach with radical, invasive surgery. Then, in the mid-1990s, an Australian doctor proved that a microscopic bacterium, not stress, causes ulcers. Now when someone is diagnosed with ulcer symptoms, doctors check for the Helicobacter pylori bacteria and then treat them with antibiotics. The same is true with low self-esteem; we have been chasing symptoms rather than addressing the true cause.

There was a time when I worked with adolescents who had been admitted to the lockup unit of a hospital. They had been placed there on a 72-hour hold for a variety of issues, including crises involving low self-esteem. Yet I am here to tell you that they were some of the most arrogant, selfish and manipulative young people I have ever encountered.

For years these teens had been either catered to and pampered or ignored and left to raise themselves. They had the earrings, tattoos, hair coloring and piercings that accompanied their self-loathing attitudes. They had stayed out all night, skipped school, taken drugs, drunk alcohol and engaged in risky sexual behavior. This self-destructiveness was actually meant to punish their parents. And when the parents tried to regain control by placing restrictions on the teens, the young people would exhibit signs of low self-esteem such as threatening to hurt themselves.

Pardon me, but give me a break!

It sounds as if they had both too much self and too much esteem. Even the Little Miss or Mister Perfect approach can be a tactic used for constant attention. In this respect, low self-esteem is demonstrated when our unrealistic expectations for perfection are not met, causing us to become angrier and angrier. We expect others to feel sorry for us and feed into our "poor me" attitude. Then, when we don't get the attention we're looking for, we can become angry, depressed and even suicidal.

I have a saying that goes like this: "Get rid of self, and there will be no esteem to worry about." As ironic as this may sound, those with low self-esteem are too focused on themselves. In an attempt to stop pains of the past or as a reward for existing in this world, they crave constant proof of their significance. They have an unquenchable appetite for others who will feed their sense of worth, and they devour attention. They eat up accolades and flattery.

In fact, they're so focused on self that it can make them easy prey. Abusers tend to look for those who need attention and lots of encouragement. They then swoop down and give this person all they're asking for and, in so doing, make for themselves a new victim.

Tonia and Richard's Story

Tonia was a 35-year-old woman who came to me because of low self-esteem issues and marriage problems. She was an engineer by trade and was well respected in her profession. She was also an attractive woman.

Her husband, Richard, was quite the opposite. He was short, overweight, and not particularly handsome. Richard was lazy and hadn't been able to keep a job. He had a problem with Internet porn, and at one point in their marriage, had convinced Tonia to participate in group sex.

Frankly, it seemed to me that Richard was the one who should have been coming in for counseling.

He recently had moved back home with Tonia after a three-month separation, during which he lived with a girlfriend he had met at his most recent job. Tonia had thrown Richard out when she found out about his girlfriend. But she continued to call Richard, using the excuse that she was calling about the kids or needed help with the plumbing, and so on. The truth, Tonia admitted, was that she wanted to check on Richard because she was jealous of his girlfriend.

"Why should you be jealous?" I asked. "He was living with another woman. Why even give him the time of day?"

"I keep thinking there's something wrong with me," Tonia replied. "Why would he want another woman? Why am I not enough? I wonder if I drove him off because of my jealousy."

As Tonia questioned herself, I was perplexed. I couldn't imagine why such an attractive, educated, talented woman would carry on this way.

"Tonia!" I said. "Why are you so concerned about him liking you? His pushing for group sex early in your marriage was enough to leave him, let alone the recent adultery. Why are you so worried about whether he rejects or accepts you? You have so much going for yourself, while he can't even keep a job. Why is it that you need his approval?"

Tears welled up in her eyes, and she said, "For years Richard told me I was nothing without him. My mother also told me I should thank Almighty God I finally found a good man and should hold onto him. I was never anything while growing up. My dad favored my sisters. Whenever anything in my life went wrong, I felt it was always my fault. Now my husband is with another woman, so I must be to blame."

After hearing the outrageous reasons Tonia had for not setting boundaries with her husband, I decided to help her understand what low self-esteem was. I told Tonia to start looking at her alleged poor image as pride and arrogance. At first, she was taken back and seemed hurt.

"How can you say that my self-esteem problem is arrogance?" She then blurted out, "My husband, mother and sisters are arrogant, not me!"

"Yes, they are arrogant," I said. "Their arrogance is overt, while yours is covert. Your arrogance developed without you ever realizing it. It sneaked up on you because of what these family members have done to you. You were conditioned to believe that you were worthless; therefore, you became very self-conscious. Now you feel that you can't afford to set boundaries or let anyone go. You need approval, assurance, and acceptance so desperately that all your focus is on you rather than what is right or true. In reality, you are self-focused."

As Tonia listened, she started letting go. She took her eyes off her false concept of need and focused on what was morally, ethically and behaviorally true. To this day, Tonia continues to write and call, thanking me for opening her eyes to the truth about her low self-esteem.

Some of you may have a difficult time with my perspective of low self-esteem, but my reply to those who suffer from it is: Try taking your eyes off yourself, and then see if you continue to stay stuck with low self-esteem.

Top 10 Ways
To Overcome Low Self-Esteem

- Remove "self" so that there's no self-esteem to worry about.

- Remove pride.

- Accept imperfection.

- Allow your imperfections to be exposed.

- Make mistakes.

- Rejoice in persecution.

- Live by grace — everything is not sin.

- Take risks.

- Remove negative friendships.

- Disregard overly critical family members.

Shame

One of childhood's most memorable Bible stories is that of Adam and Eve. We remember that when Eve ate the forbidden fruit, her husband tagged right along! Well, the story doesn't end there. It goes on to say that Adam and Eve, feeling naked and ashamed, covered themselves by sewing fig leaves together and then hid when they heard God coming.

According to this famous Bible story, God called out to Adam, and when Adam answered, God asked him, "Who told you that you were naked? Have you eaten from the tree that I commanded you not to eat from?" Of course, Adam blamed Eve by saying, "It was that woman you gave me." Eve then blamed the serpent! It appears that shame causes us not only to hide, but to blame others as well. This story is a good illustration of what shame is and what it does to us.

Some people feel they are wrong, whether or not they're guilty, and the result is shame. Shame makes a person feel naked and exposed, and anyone filled with it will try to cover up. They will find a way to hide or isolate themselves from the source that might expose their secret. No one likes to reveal his or her dirty laundry.

Those reared in a shame-filled environment have knee-jerk reactions to anyone who comes too close to whatever ugly, black secret they've kept hidden for years. These secrets include sexual or emotional abuse, personal failures, inner inadequacies, family embarrassments, or anything else that may have made them feel dirty.

Even though these self-protective individuals gravitate toward a spouse or companion whom they consider safe, they often sabotage the relationship because of the supposed darkness in their own soul. People filled with shame will react angrily if their partner gets too close for comfort. They will attack or withdraw in order to protect their shameful secret at all costs.

Remember, the only way to get angry is through an unmet expectation. Shame-based individuals have an unspoken expectation that says, "Don't get too close or I might get hurt." They expect loved ones to:

1. be devoted to them unconditionally without exposing their ugly secret, and
2. to fix the nagging self-contempt with which they live without ever probing or revealing the real issue.

Because shame-based people feel they must keep others at a distance, it can be very difficult to develop an intimate relationship with them. They seem constantly angry and depressed over what their spouse, family and friends are supposedly doing to them, when the reality is they're angry about the secret they are protecting. It is a slick, subtle way of sewing fig leaves together and hiding among the foliage!

Brent and Mindy's Story

Brent called me for counseling after hearing my radio program on the subject of shame. During the first session, Brent shared that his wife, Mindy, had stopped sleeping in the same bedroom with him about two years earlier. He said his wife was chronically disappointed and angry with him, to the point that he had joined church groups, quit jobs, and moved several times to appease her.

"I tried and tried to make her happy," Brent said. "But things deteriorated quickly, and I'd given up hope. When I heard you explain about the repercussions of shame, I realized you were describing what might be wrong with my wife."

I pointed out Brent's codependency issue toward Mindy and was able to show him how to stop catering to her manipulation. Even though counseling that employs a direct approach was a new concept to Brent, I told him it was important that he encourage his wife to come in to see me. The best way to do this, I explained, was to let Mindy think she would be coming in order to help *him*. You see, shame-based spouses are usually more likely to come for counseling if they think it's their other half who needs the help.

Mindy consented. I began the session by reading her background information and noticed she had answered the question about past abuse with a question mark. I am amazed how many counselees aren't sure what actually constitutes abuse. Mindy was one of them. She admitted she really didn't know if she had been abused or not. Her response indicated to me she was trying to avoid the reality of her past.

I asked Mindy to explain her answer. The more I asked about that particular question, the more she became defensive.

"Why are you asking me these questions? I thought we were meeting about my husband," she said. Her response was one typical of people filled with shame. I reworded my questions so that she could feel safe enough to share her story. Finally, tears began to flow down her cheeks.

"This has nothing to do with our marriage," she protested in a weepy voice. "My husband is just insensitive to me. That's why we're not close."

Mindy continued to justify herself and blame her husband, emitting a rage that was the result of her own self-hatred.

Finally, after I had allowed her to vent for about 20 minutes, I leaned toward her and asked, "If he is as bad as you say he is, why don't you just divorce him?"

"Well, sometimes he is okay. Plus, what would our children think?"

"What does it matter what your children think?" I replied. "If he is that bad, then the chaos is destroying you and the children anyway."

With a blank stare on her face, she sat quietly, tears rolling down her face.

I broke the silence. "Why don't you tell me what really happened to you when you were a little girl? Who hurt you?"

This time, she broke into a loud and uncontrollable sob and then began to repeat over and over how much she hated her dad. It turns out that Mindy's father had sexually abused her when she was 12 years old. Her mother never addressed it and kept silent, living in denial.

Mindy's shame manifested itself in the form of blame, which she aimed at her husband. Fearful of exposing the deep hurt and darkness in her own soul, Mindy attacked Brent and isolated herself.

This is the same kind of "blame game" Adam and Eve played more than 6,000 years ago.

As I indicated earlier, individuals with shame-based anger usually attack the one closest to them. The person nearest their door of darkness and secrecy will feel the brunt of their rage.

The lasting effects of shame may be why you are stuck in your relationship and why love is not enough.

Top 10 Ways to Identify a Shame-Based Life

• Avoiding people who know too much about them.

• Repeated failed relationships.

• Tendency to lie in order to protect themselves.

• Contempt, hate, and rage toward others and self.

• Fear of intimacy — keeping loved ones at bay and punishing them if they get too close.

• Feelings of dread and anxiety.

• Perfectionist lifestyle.

• Difficulty receiving constructive criticism.

• Extreme emotions (ups and downs).

• Difficulty receiving unconditional love and forgiveness from God or man.

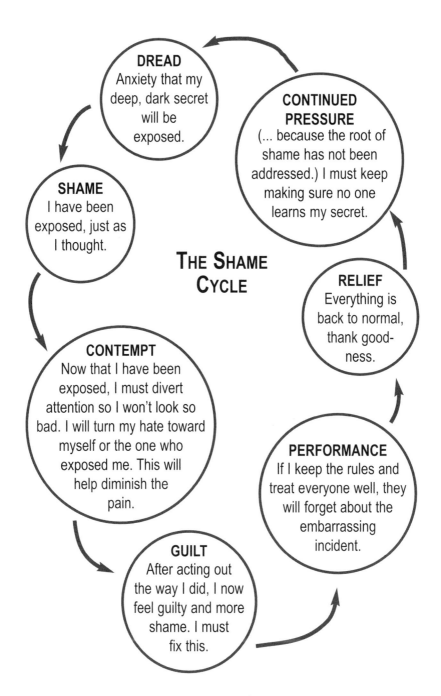

DREAD
Anxiety that my deep, dark secret will be exposed.

CONTINUED PRESSURE
(... because the root of shame has not been addressed.) I must keep making sure no one learns my secret.

SHAME
I have been exposed, just as I thought.

THE SHAME CYCLE

RELIEF
Everything is back to normal, thank goodness.

CONTEMPT
Now that I have been exposed, I must divert attention so I won't look so bad. I will turn my hate toward myself or the one who exposed me. This will help diminish the pain.

PERFORMANCE
If I keep the rules and treat everyone well, they will forget about the embarrassing incident.

GUILT
After acting out the way I did, I now feel guilty and more shame. I must fix this.

Top 10 Ways to Break the Shame Cycle

1. Face the truth about yourself — the good, the bad and the ugly.

2. Understand that all things can work together for the good.

3. Learn not to fear what others think of you.

4. Expose your shame.

5. Learn what shame statements are, and refuse to accept or use them.

6. Surround yourself with positive, trustworthy and encouraging people.

7. Recognize that shame is a form of arrogance and unhealthy self-centeredness.

8. Expect rejection from those who would try to shame you when you set boundaries with them.

9. Invest in your recovery.

10. Rather than Adam and Eve's nakedness, identify with Christ's; Jesus was unclothed and exposed on the cross, but he did not react out of shame.

Chapter 7

Personality Disorders

As I mentioned earlier, there can be more profound reasons why people stay in a constant state of anger, and some of them can be devastatingly difficult to detect. Even diagnosable mood disorders such as bipolar can go undetected for years before a family member or spouse suspects it. Even so, I would say mood disorders tend to reveal themselves much more quickly than personality disorders.

Individuals with a genuine personality disorder may have no idea they have one. A personality disorder can act like a stealth bomber that delivers one bomb after another, destroying not only their intended targets but leaving a wide swath of collateral damage! Close family and friends often don't know what hit them until years later. Individuals with personality disorders can blend in with society so easily that most people outside their family may think the complaining friends and relatives are crazy.

The DSM lists 10 personality disorders, which are grouped into three clusters:

1. Cluster A (odd or eccentric disorders):
   - Paranoid personality disorder
   - Schizoid personality disorder
   - Schizotypal personality disorder
2. Cluster B (dramatic, emotional or erratic disorders):
   - Antisocial personality disorder
   - Borderline personality disorder
   - Histrionic personality disorder
   - Narcissistic personality disorder
3. Cluster C (anxious or fearful disorders):
   - Avoidant personality disorder
   - Dependent personality disorder
   - Obsessive-compulsive personality disorder (not the same as obsessive-compulsive disorder)

While 10 personality disorders are listed in the DSM, I am only going to expound on the four that I see most often in my practice.

Dependent Personality Disorder

Experts describe dependent personality disorder as a pervasive psychological dependence on other people. What the difference is between a dependent personality and a dependent personality disorder is something mental health professionals have not quite agreed upon. This, of course, means that diagnoses vary from one case to another. As you will read later on, some people have a dependent nature that no one will ever change. You will also see that being dependent isn't necessarily bad.

According to the DSM, dependent personality disorder is defined as a pervasive and excessive need to be taken care of that leads to submissive and clinging behavior and fears of separation. This disorder can begin by early adulthood and appears in a variety of contexts, as indicated by five or more of the following:

- Difficulty making everyday decisions without an excessive amount of advice and reassurance from others.

- A need for others to assume responsibility for most major areas of life.

- Difficulty expressing disagreement with others because of fear of loss of support or approval. (This does not include realistic fears of retribution.)

- Difficulty initiating projects or doing things on their own because of a lack of self-confidence in judgment or ab-ilities rather than a lack of motivation or energy.

- Going to excessive lengths to obtain nurturance and support from others, to the point of volunteering to do things that are unpleasant.

- Discomfort or helplessness when alone because of an exaggerated fear of being unable to care for themselves.

- Urgently seeking another relationship as a source of care and support when a close relationship ends.
- Unrealistically preoccupied with fears of being left to take care of themselves.

Dependence Deciphered

The DSM includes the following mnemonic that can be used to remember the criteria for dependent personality disorder:

D – Difficulty making everyday decisions.

E – Excessive lengths to obtain nurturance and support from others.

P – Preoccupied with fears of being left to fend for themselves.

E – Exaggerated fears of being unable to care for themselves.

N – Needs others to assume responsibility for their life.

D – Difficulty expressing disagreement with others.

E – End of one close relationship demands they begin another.

N – Noticeable difficulties in initiating projects or doing things on their own.

T – "Take care of me" is their motto.

Problems Caused by Dependence

Because of their excessive need for approval, people afflicted with a dependent personality disorder will try hard to please others. In fact, they can try so hard they become frustrated when they feel forced to do things they don't want to and unable to express their true feelings about it. Furthermore, their clinging behavior can make close relationships difficult to establish and maintain.

When these relationships end, individuals with DPD will feel desperate and unable to take care of themselves. People with DPD also often have very low self-esteem and are vulnerable to other mental disorders, especially depression and anxiety.

This description of DPD could also describe an inborn temperament called the supine. The National Christian Counselors Association, along with its founder, Dr. Richard Arno, conducted an 11-year study with 1,000 people to determine the validity and effects of inborn temperaments. We will take an in-depth look at temperament in a later chapter, but here we'll look at the supine temperament as it relates to dependency.

According to the NCCA study, one particular group of people did not possess any of the characteristics believed to be the original four inborn temperament types, traceable back to the time of Hippocrates (460-370 BC). These four types of temperament are sanguine, melancholy, choleric and phlegmatic.

But the NCCA study identified a fifth temperament type, the supine, in which the person behaves like the introverted melancholy but also responds like the outgoing, extroverted sanguine.

They found that people who consistently showed these characteristics were those who demonstrated indirect behavior. This means that they act as if they *don't* want what deep inside they really *do*! For instance, they act as if they don't want to socialize when they really do. They behave as if they don't want your love, approval or affection when they actually do.

Individuals with this temperament love to give, serve, and please others. They tend to be followers, not leaders. They love to be the support person, not the one in charge. They don't like to make decisions by themselves but need to be included in the decision-making process. Because the supine temperament is naturally giving and compliant, they can easily become the victims of selfish and controlling people.

As a Professional Clinical Member of the National Christian Counselors Association, I am certified to administer the clinical test that determines an individual's temperament type. When clients score as a supine in the area of control, I know immediately what needs to be done in order to help them. I don't look at dependency as simply a disorder, but as a natural, inborn temperament that is part of someone's genetic makeup.

This does not mean someone who is a supine can't use their natural temperament in a dysfunctional manner; it does mean that they can control their dependency better once they understand the needs of their temperament.

I have discovered that when I advise supine individuals to stop allowing others to hurt them, they often became even more dependent and panicky. Supines do not like to fight; in fact, they don't like to hurt anyone, even their enemies. Their instincts tell them the world should be a kinder and gentler place. Rather than suggest supines behave differently than they're being compelled to by their temperament, I've found it's better to educate them on how to attract safe people who understand and care for them.

The problem is that most other temperament types don't know how to properly handle supine dependency. We tend to take advantage of supines' weakness, then turn around and expect them to be independent and strong-willed. This causes a supine to become confused and hurt. When they are hurt over and over again for a long period of time, they often shut down and retreat. Once they have reached the point of running away from us, they're virtually impossible to win back.

My goal as a counselor is to help those with dependency disorders accept their inborn temperaments and demonstrate their God-given qualities in a healthy manner. In order not to stay stuck in dysfunction and abuse, those with dependency disorders must learn to depend on trustworthy people.

What is codependency?

Codependency is a word to describe someone who enables or continually excuses another person's unacceptable behavior. Another way to define codependency is "feeding into" the behavior of an individual who is causing pain and stress to the unit as a whole. Units can be the workplace, school, social clubs, church and, of course, the family.

Many times codependents will develop self-destructive habits of their own in order to deal with the frustration of being unable to stand up for what they know is right. These displaced habits can be in the form of overeating, under-eating, drinking, self-isolation, sex, excessive attention to detail (obsessive-compulsive disorder, or OCD), excessive obedience, and even self-mutilation. Codependents are often filled with self-contempt and do self-destructive things rather than risk losing the approval of a loved one.

Can dependency be good?

As part of the human race, we all need each other in order to survive as a society. We depend on one another in order to become successful in our jobs, careers and relationships. Married couples must depend on each other to be successful in rearing children and running a household. In other words, to depend on others is a must for survival. The question about codependency is not one of whether we should depend on those who are close to us or help one another accomplish common goals that are benefiting the whole. Rather, the question should be: Are we appeasing a person who is being disruptive just so we won't be rejected or challenged?

If you're walking on eggshells to avoid repercussions, then you're in the clutches of codependency. Most relationship problems stem from this unhealthy behavior. Many times codependent behavior escalates like a snowball that becomes an avalanche before being dealt with appropriately. By that time, the one seeking help can feel overwhelmed by codependency's devastating effects. However, there is hope! It is never too late to get the help you need and to make a positive change.

Where did the word codependency originate?

In the early to mid-1970s, many healthcare professionals discovered that addicts seeking treatment for their abuse of alcohol or drugs were not the only ones to blame for their habitual behaviors.

They found that loved ones, friends and coworkers help, or enable, addicts to continue their unhealthy habits by failing to confront them, fearing the addict's blame, anger and rejection.

After discovering that family members and friends can be co-conspirators in the addict's demise, mental health workers and doctors coined the term "codependent." Medical professionals soon found that, in some cases, codependents could be more difficult to deal with than the actual alcoholic or drug addict. Much later they also noted that codependent behaviors prevailed through many generations.

At St. John's Chemical Dependency Program in Salina, KS, an article was written that defined codependency as: "a set of maladaptive, compulsive behaviors learned by family members in order to survive in a family which is experiencing great emotional pain and stress." It goes on to explain that these behaviors are passed from generation to generation, whether or not alcohol or drugs are actually present. The original addict may have been the great, great grandfather of a family currently suffering the repercussions of his codependent behavior.

What happens is that family members who lived with the great, great grandfather learned to use a set of behaviors that helped them deal with the emotional pain and stress of living with him. I call this kind of behavior an "elaborate coping mechanism." As a desperate means of self-preservation, codependents instinctively develop elaborate coping mechanisms.

Unfortunately, the behaviors themselves are habit-forming and destructive and so must be broken. As an athlete trains to recondition themselves through repetitive workouts, so the codependent must learn to say "no," "I will not," "I can't," and "I refuse" to the person who is using, abusing, manipulating, and controlling them.

Dale's Story

A friend told me I needed to talk with a man named Dale about his situation. I made an appointment to have lunch with Dale, and we weren't far into our meal before I found myself engrossed in the sad story of the 64-year-old former minister. I listened to him intently until almost dinnertime.

Dale was a minister who had planted several churches and spent most of his life trying to help people. He had a temperament that was very supine (dependent) in the area of control, and very sanguine (outgoing) in the area of affection. Growing up on a farm where life was simple and ingenuous, Dale from a young age was taught that just about everything outside of church life was a sin. Even though Dale developed a normal drive toward the opposite sex, he was plagued with shame for having such desires.

Through the years I have seen many strict Christian parents use the Bible to instill shame and fear in their children. This type of teaching is based, not on a proper interpretation of the Bible, but upon the fears and mistakes parents have suffered in their own lives. It can cause a child to make shame-based decisions that, for the rest of their lives, lead to fear, guilt and failed relationships. Many Christians believe that if they have a strong sex drive, they should get married ASAP rather than burn with sinful lust. It's a flawed philosophy that causes long-term problems.

Dale was one of those children caught in the web of false "Christian" guilt. He married a Christian girl whom he thought would be pleasing to God and his parents — especially his parents. She was not, however, the type Dale would have picked for himself. Yet because of his dependent nature, Dale did and said what he was told, not what he truly wanted.

Early in his marriage, Dale learned that his wife did not have much of a sex drive. Like Dale, she was raised to believe sex was dirty and bad, and she would withdraw from him for weeks — sometimes months. She even had difficulty showing simple affection.

Having a dependent personality, Dale then fell prey to a woman in his congregation who gladly met his sexual drive. He divorced his wife of almost 20 years and married this woman from his flock who appeared to share his sexual desire. He stepped down as minister and would never again hold a position as senior pastor. People with a dependent personality, coupled with a shame-based upbringing, will eventually fall victim to an opportunist.

At the age of 40 and after fathering three children with his first wife and having one child with his second, Dale decided to get a vasectomy. When he went in for the simple surgery of snipping the two vas deferens tubes that supply sperm, he heard the doctor say: "I think we have a problem here." When Dale heard those words, he figured the doctor had found he had some sort of incurable disease. But what the doctor said was: "I think you have more than two tubes in your scrotum." Dale did not have three tubes. Neither did he have four. He had *five* vas deferens tubes. Five pressure points that caused him to be not only very fertile, but to be capable of multiple orgasms. There was a medical reason Dale had such a strong sex drive. All those vas deferens tubes were the real enemy, not his sinful nature.

After the vasectomy, Dale's new wife started working for another minister. And … you guessed it. She behaved with him just as she had with Dale, eventually running off with the man. This is not uncommon. I would estimate that more insecure, dependent ministers per capita are committing adultery than their lay population.

Dale was experiencing his second failed relationship, but he soon met another woman at church. Unfortunately, there are many lonely, church-going women all too glad to fill whatever spot becomes available. The woman Dale had recently met was by far the most sexually aggressive, meeting all of Dale's needs in the physical sense. Because of his inborn temperament and his five vas deferens tubes, Dale was vulnerable to a sexually aggressive woman with a premeditated agenda. Dale fell for the bait and married her. Soon after the wedding, she began lying, cheating, stealing his money, and even beating him. Then her sexual aggression came to a halt, and she became frigid. After months of this, Dale probed into her background and found she had a history of this type of behavior.

Sadly, this is not the end of Dale's story. After Dale divorced this woman, he started rebuilding his life once more. Months went by. It's difficult for people with dependent personalities to be alone for long periods because they feel they should be with someone in order to be happy and fulfilled. It was the same for Dale. About this time he got a phone call from his third wife, the woman who had just about ruined his life.

"What's going on?" she asked, in the sweet tone she knew Dale had a soft spot for.

"Things are finally settling down after the divorce," he answered. And that's when his ex-wife started crying. Remember earlier when I explained how to make a list before returning to a destructive relationship? Well, Dale hadn't gotten these instructions yet, and his dependent, needy nature took over as he allowed her to plead her case for getting back into his good graces.

Individuals with a supine temperament or a dependent personality have to understand they must not talk to, listen to, or sympathize with anyone who all but devastates their lives. Because supines will always be vulnerable to emotional words, they must just hang up or walk away.

Dale's ex-wife had called, not because she loved him, but because she had been rejected by her most recent lover and was broke and desperate. But she told Dale everything he wanted to hear. Promising to make up for all the terrible wrongs she had committed against him, she convinced Dale to take her back. Once again she poured sex and affection on him, and Dale remarried her. Then, as you might expect, the repeat offender started her invasion all over again. She ran Dale's credit card up to $85,000, cut him off sexually, and began to physically attack him as part of her plan to set him up on domestic violence charges.

It worked. One day she started hitting and punching Dale, backing him into a corner, where she tried to knee him in the groin area. Reflexively, he blocked her across the thighs as she delivered the blow. She leaped over to the phone and dialed 911, telling police that Dale had attacked her. After officers saw the bruises on her legs, they arrested Dale.

Sitting in jail for the first time in his life, Dale was devastated. He knew nothing about the judicial system, domestic violence charges or being put on a sex offender list for the rest of his life. He spent three days in jail before his brother bailed him out.

Dale's wife, who had a long history of abusing him and had just viciously attacked him, acted as if she were sorry and hired an attorney — with Dale's credit card — to defend him. The attorney she hired, however, was one she knew would do a poor job. It was a setup.

On the advice of his lawyer, Dale pleaded guilty to a lesser charge. He was given probation but is now a registered sex offender unable to get a job with any business that does background checks. Dale can no longer be a minister, bus driver, factory worker, etc. For this the lawyer charged him $30,000.

Dale's naiveté and overly dependent nature triggered a domino effect that not only kept him stuck in his behavioral healing but caused irreparable damage that will follow him into old age.

If you have dysfunctional dependency issues, Dale's story is one that should encourage you to get help before you too make the same mistake over and over again. Below is a guide to breaking codependency and dependency disorder.

Top 10 Actions for Breaking Codependency

1. **Learn to pay attention to your doubts and premonitions.** Self-doubt is common for those suffering the effects of codependency. They feel others are always right, while they are usually wrong. Because a codependent longs to please their loved ones, they rarely ask questions, even if foul play is suspected. They feel it's safer not to doubt or question their loved one because they're conditioned to think they're wrong. But a codependent person must pay attention to their doubts and premonitions, and when they feel something is wrong, they should seek out confirmation and encouragement from a trusted and trained counselor.

2. **Do not allow emotions — either yours or someone else's — sway your stance on a matter.** Codependents have difficulty deciphering the difference between a person who genuinely needs their help and

one who is only using them. Why? Because codependents need to be loved and accepted at all cost. Perpetrators prey on that need with emotional weaponry. For instance, if a codependent suspects they are being used and stops giving to the other person, the perpetrator will attempt to manipulate them. These users often have an incredible knack for exploiting emotions in order to make a codependent family member or friend feel guilty. Sometimes they target a weaker family member in order to get money, favors and support for a bad habit. Many times they shed real tears while telling a lie intended to make others feel sorry for them. They bring over their children to tug on heartstrings. They promise their undying love and devotion if only the codependent will give into their demands. These opportunists will also threaten to withhold love and approval if their demands aren't met. Mothers and grandmothers, because of their nurturing disposition, are especially vulnerable to this kind of abuse. Numerous times, when someone has shared with me how they feel stuck in their marriage, they relate that the reason they married their spouse was that when they tried to end the relationship, their partner cried, threw a fit or threatened suicide. But take my advice: Never marry a person you feel you can't break up with. Believe me, they are not as heartbroken or as dependent as they say they are! And even if they *were* as dependent as they would have you believe, then that's all the more reason not to marry them! If you are codependent, you'll save yourself a good deal of trouble if you take this to heart: Never make a decision based on emotions. No matter how much you're being pressured, wait at least 24 hours and consult with a counselor and/or trusted family member who isn't interested in placating the person playing on your emotions. (By the way, this principle also applies when deciding whether to make a purchase.)

3. **Trust your gut.** In truth, gut feelings are rarely wrong. However, it is very important for the person who is breaking the clutches of codependency to know the difference between gut feelings and emotions. Codependents are usually very confused about the difference between honest intuition and emotionalism. Having conditioned themselves to think they are usually wrong, they no longer trust their gut. But a gut feeling is an internal detection device that warns you when things don't quite measure up. For example, you know that if you give a toddler a knife, they're likely to hurt themselves. In the same way, you know that, even when your spouse tells you this is the last time they'll drink, they will do so again. You can trust your gut. Unfortunately, codependents ignore these inner danger signals, accepting instead the emotional pleas being hurled at them. They continue to hope for the best based on the emotions the other person is displaying rather than the truth they know in their gut.

4. Do not agree just to agree. Have you ever known someone who seemed to agree with everyone, even though you suspected they really didn't believe a word being said? You're probably envisioning a super slick salesperson — or a real, live codependent! Most codependents are so afraid of confrontation and rejection that they'll agree to just about anything in order to keep the peace. Confronted with an aggressive, overbearing person, they agree with them in hopes that they will settle down and no one will get hurt. Codependents also believe that the aggressor will see the error of their ways and then everyone will live happily ever after! A nice fairytale, but not necessarily true. The codependent may momentarily diffuse things, but the long-range message the perpetrator gets is that their bullying behavior works! My advice to the codependent is: Agree only when you totally believe something is true. This will require that you restructure the way you think, which may take some time. It might also be a good idea to spend some of that time with a counselor who understands codependency.

5. Do not fear repercussions when you confront others. Codependents are under the illusion that everyone should be happy all the time, and that they should not experience any conflict in life. But when we set boundaries, it many times ignites insecurities in the other person, and they may threaten divorce, retaliation, withholding their love, cutting us off financially, and other emotional manipulations usually so effective on codependents. In order for codependents to break through their fear of repercussions, they must learn how to recondition their thinking. They need to understand that when they give into threats, they only make matters worse. I regularly see adults still dealing with the frustration of having parents who tried to keep the peace with a dysfunctional family member. The counselee, who as a child was obedient and compliant, as an adult often demonstrates rage because while they were growing up, a parent failed to set appropriate boundaries. It may have been a trouble-making sibling, an abusive parent, or an intrusive relative who was never confronted with their mistreatment of the "good" kid. Instead, the parent gave more attention to the disruptive family member and ignored the obedient one, actually punishing the good behavior and rewarding the bad. Meanwhile, the codependent parent thought they were catering to both sides. But it's as Aneurin Bevan, a British politician, once said: "We know what happens to people who stay in the middle of the road. They get run over." In order not to get run over, codependents need to stop worrying about other people's reactions and set healthy boundaries.

6. **Examine your doubts with the help of a professional.**
   Why should a codependent see a professional? For the

simple reason that codependents tend to believe everyone, and, when they must choose, usually go with
whomever sounds the most convincing at the moment.
Regrettably, many times this person is the very one causing the problem in the first place. That's why it's important
for the codependent to have a neutral, non-biased view of
the situation. Hopefully, the counselor or professional
whom they have selected will be one who exhibits wisdom and integrity.

7. **Do not be controlled by others who use Scripture.**
Because codependents view God and the Bible through
the tainted window of shame, guilt and manipulation, they
are easily controlled by a fear of what God would think if
they happened to step out of bounds. This is why it is
easy for family and friends to persuade the codependent
to conform to their views, simply by using assumed biblical principles and skewed Scriptures. Using the Bible to
get one's way has been a manipulative art since the first
century. It's been invoked by power-hungry pastors,
priests who needed to cover secret sins, megalomaniac
cult leaders, husbands trying to regain their manhood,
and wives trying to convince their husband to love them.
The list of insecure perpetrators goes on and on. It is very
important for a codependent to understand that just
because someone can quote the Bible, it doesn't make
them right.

8. **Be selfish when it comes to making the right decisions.** Somehow many of us have gotten the idea that people who set boundaries, say "no," stand against injustice, and take care of themselves are selfish people. From the cradle, many of us have been taught to obey and never question. Some of us have never quite made it through that rite of passage known as rebellious adolescence, which is so important in establishing independence. Even though teens can drive parents crazy, there is real purpose in going through this oppositional, defiant stage because it transforms dependent, frightened, controlled children into adults capable of making confident decisions on their own. It is a stage, which — if properly nurtured — will break a person of continuing in abnormal dependency, and it's called growing up. Some parents subdue their teen with so much fear that the child becomes confused, afraid that making decisions apart from their parent is selfish. Actually, people who act meek, timid, compliant to manipulation, and cooperative with abusers are usually selfish themselves. Their codependency helps them avoid feeling bad. They appear to be self-sacrificing, but they're really trying to spare their own feelings. Codependents need to be selfish when it comes to doing what is right, rather than doing whatever happens to be easiest.

9. Do not accept blame or admit wrong just to avoid a confrontation. As I mentioned, codependents avoid conflict at all cost. In their quest to create a perfect world, codependents will take mud in the face so they don't have to feel the embarrassment of someone else who might really have needed the mudpack facial! Some codependent spouses will take the blame for their alcoholic mate. Some have taken the rap for a domestic violence arrest. Some have even allowed a spouse to commit child abuse and then blamed themselves. In order to truly break the shackles of codependency, its victims must stop playing the sacrificial lamb. Such a role is reprehensible because it covers up someone else's crime, hurts the innocent, and never creates genuine peace.

10. Stop rescuing others from their problems. I have what I call "Tom Joseph's Eleventh Commandment." It states, "Thou shall not have an intimate relationship with anyone you will have to rescue, save or fix." Many codependents look for mates who have something broken in their lives. Believe me when I say this: You can develop a serious relationship with that kind of victim, but it will never work in the long run. If you genuinely want to help that person, you must be strong enough to forego any intimate involvement with them until they have fully recovered from their situation and a significant period of time has passed. Many men and women make wretched relational decisions thinking they can keep a sentimental dream alive by rescuing a certain someone from their woes. Men may see themselves as a hero rescuing a damsel in distress, but the reality in such situations is that they are opportunists seizing the chance to be hailed as someone's savior. It might be a Cinderella story, but not in the way we would like to believe. In fact, I've often wondered how the fairytale would have turned out if the story had continued after the prince married Cinderella. What a tragic tale that would have been as the prince was forced to deal with the emotional baggage from Cindy's dysfunctional step-family and her many abuse and abandonment issues! There are red flags that codependents should not take lightly. They include: a family history of mental problems, violent abuse, financial irresponsibility, addictions, and a victim mentality. These issues create pain and problems with irreparable consequences.

Top 10 Red Flags

1. Domestic violence of any kind in their background.

2. Addictions of any kind. Problems (past or present) with substance abuse.

3. Bankruptcy, debts, and other financial problems.

4. The mental, emotional and behavioral condition of their dependent children.

5. Past marital status: Have they been divorced? Why?

How many times? Have they been single for a prolonged period of time? Have they lived with anyone, and how many times?

6. Condition of the family of origin: poverty, mental illnesses, abuses, religious background, alcoholism, instances of suicide.

7. Criminal record.

8. Obliviousness to their inborn temperament.

9. Sexual abuse, either as a victim or perpetrator.

10. Hospitalization, diagnosis or treatment for a mental, mood or personality disorder of any kind.

Chapter 8

Obsessive-Compulsive Personality Disorder

While many people have heard of obsessive-compulsive disorder, or OCD, I've found that few have heard of obsessive-compulsive *personality* disorder, or OCPD. While the names are similar, the conditions are actually quite different. Those who suffer from OCPD do not generally feel the need to perform repetitive, ritualistic actions such as excessive hand washing, vacuuming, cleaning, and counting stairs, which can be common with OCD. Instead, people with OCPD tend to stress perfectionism above all else and feel anxious when they perceive that things are not "right."

OCPD is characterized by perfectionism, excessive orderliness, and a generally inflexible conformity to rules and procedures. People with OCPD may hoard money, keep

104

their home perfectly organized, and have a difficult time delegating tasks in the fear they won't be done correctly. They may even adopt rituals like the typical OCD sufferer. But those with OCPD think in terms of black and white; they believe people are either completely right or absolutely wrong. As might be expected, their excessive demands can make relating to them difficult, especially for those closest to them.

According to the DSM, obsessive-compulsive personality disorder is a "pervasive pattern of preoccupation with orderliness, perfectionism, mental and interpersonal control, at the expense of flexibility and openness." It begins by early adulthood and presents itself in a variety of contexts, as indicated by four or more of the following:

- Preoccupation with details, rules, lists, order, organization, bodily functions or schedules to the extent that the major point of the activity is lost.

- Showing perfectionism that interferes with task completion (e.g., is unable to complete a project because his or her own overly-strict standards are not met).

- Excessive devotion to work and productivity to the exclusion of leisure activities and friendships (not accounted for by obvious economic necessity).

- Being overly conscientious, scrupulous and inflexible about matters of morality, ethics or values (not accounted for by cultural or religious identification).

- Inability to discard worn-out or worthless objects even when they have no sentimental value.

- Reluctance to delegate tasks or to work with others unless they submit to exactly his or her way of doing things.

- Adopting a miserly spending style toward both self and others; money is viewed as something to be hoarded for future catastrophes.

- Showing rigidity and stubbornness.

The OCPD clients I see often mimic the selfish behaviors of a narcissist. (See Chapter 10 on narcissistic personality disorder.) A title I use to describe someone with OCPD is:

The Socially Accepted Dictator

It was the first time I met Jack, my soon-to-be father-in-law. His gray hair was flawlessly combed, his home was in perfect order, and he seemed very open and accepting. I was surprised when, on the way home, my fiancé (and now wife), Vicki, seemed distant and upset.

"What's wrong?" I asked.

"He's good at first impressions, but you just don't know him."

I was a little taken aback because her father seemed to have raised her in a good home with all the necessary provisions, but Vicki insisted she always felt uncomfortable around him. She longed for his acceptance and love, she said, but she also disliked him. I was a bit shocked that she would feel so about her own father.

Through the years, however, I've had ample opportunity to see what Vicki meant. Each time our children visited Grandpa, he would be very critical of them. They couldn't spill their drink, mess up the rugs, or leave smudge marks on the sliding glass door. He would condemn them just for being kids and doing the things kids do. Once they were grown, they remarked: "Grandpa Jack was a mean grandfather."

Jack tended to correct Vicki's mom in front of everyone by using degrading and condescending remarks and would often shut her down when she wanted to contribute to family discussions. After many disappointments, we decided not to visit Vicki's parents unless something drastically changed.

Jack was a World War II veteran who had retired as an executive with a nationally known oil company after 35 years. The company may have valued him, but I remember the contempt he held for his coworkers. He once mentioned to me that he had a stiff back from the night before.

"Oh yeah?" I asked.

"Yes," he said. "Last night I had a dream I was punching some of those idiots I use to work with, and I found myself falling out of bed and onto the floor."

Vicki told me that while she was growing up, her father would rant about his coworkers every night over dinner, which he expected on the table at exactly 5 p.m. Their house had to be deep-cleaned every Saturday, even if things were already spotless. She remembered a time when her father had to go to the doctor because he had scrubbed his skin so hard while showering that it had become enflamed.

Says Vicki: "No one could make a mistake in my home. Our house was like a funeral home. Everything was perfect and hermetically sealed."

I remember the first time I saw Jack's garage. The floor was painted, and all the tools were arranged neatly by size and weight. All his keys were hung, each with its own typed label affixed nearby.

He once gave us an old Honda with 120,000 miles on it in order to get a tax writeoff. He also gave us the vehicle's maintenance file, which contained information about every oil change, every light bulb replaced, and every dime spent on the car. While it was great to have that information, I had to ask Vicki, "Does your dad have a life?" She laughed a little and cried a little, too, and, as she wiped away the tears, said: "He was always angry and filled with rage toward me. Growing up with him was hell."

Jack had OCPD. Like others with the disorder, he was so dominating and angry that it was almost impossible for him to coexist closely with others. For instance, he was just fine when he communicated via email or phone, but whenever we invaded his germ-free bubble with a visit, he treated us like intruders. After I pointed this out to Vicki, she could see very clearly that her father had indeed forged an imaginary bubble around himself and his living space. Whenever visitors left his home, he would clean whatever they had touched and would rake the fringes on the throw rugs that had been displaced. He had to have total control over his environment. The only time he was halfway normal was when he self-medicated with alcohol. This is why people suffering from this problem can very easily become an alcoholic or drug addict. Frankly, sometimes they're easier to live with when they're sedated.

Oftentimes OCPD can be helped with antidepressants and/or anti-anxiety medications. The only problem is getting them to take the medication because they never accept the fact that they need it. The way they live is the right way, they believe, and everyone else has it wrong.

My father-in-law was so obsessive that when he died in 2005, he had his obituary written out and had arranged his funeral so that no one could attend. He died a lonely, angry man. He left all his money and possessions to a family member who exhibits the same OCPD patterns. Vicki had to grieve for her loss and her father's rejection while giving herself permission to be angry. Then she had to move on. OCPD is another condition that can make family members wonder why we stay stuck.

OCPD and Sexual Deviancy

In every overtly OCPD case I've counseled, the counselee was involved in some kind of sexual immorality or bizarre sexual addiction such as sadomasochism. After much thought, I have concluded that these perfectionists put so much pressure on themselves to keep everything orderly that they resort to risky and outrageous sexual acts as an outlet.

Kevin's Story

A lady named Rachel once approached me about counseling her family. She was handling all the problems at home because her husband's job kept him out of town most of the time. Their teenage son was depressed and having some issues at school, and their daughter was rebellious.

Our first counseling session set off a series of events that eventually changed the course of Rachel's life. In that first session, I found that Rachel's children had no respect for her and took nothing she said seriously. They had been schooled by their father, Kevin, to believe their mother was stupid, without any common sense about her. I also learned that Kevin had complete control of the family finances, never revealing any information about them to Rachel. Meanwhile, Rachel suffered from dependent disorders and codependent issues, having grown up in an environment that prepared her to succumb to abusive, condescending and controlling behavior.

After evaluating the family dynamics, I knew I had to meet with Kevin. He explained that he had been living and working out of town for the last two years of his marriage, seeing the family two weekends a month. I told Kevin that it would be better if he could transfer back to be with his family. "They really need you," I said.

Kevin eventually moved back, and, as I continued to counsel Rachel and Kevin, I could see that Kevin exhibited strong signs of OCPD, which likely was at the root of their children's' problems. The family didn't recognize his overbearing nature because he hadn't lived with them most of the time. Kevin knew that living alone, away from his family, would help him cope with the stress of children who were out of order, a wife who had emotional problems, and a home that was not perfect.

But the most crucial part of this story involves Kevin's sexual fantasies. For most of his adult life, Kevin had indulged heavily in pornography. During intercourse with his wife, Kevin would force Rachel to engage in degrading and painful acts. In couples counseling, Kevin would agree to honor his wife's wishes and not engage in the kind of sex that humiliated her. But someone who is involved with an addiction like his — and especially one who shows signs of OCPD — cannot just decide one day to quit.

After Kevin had been home living with his family awhile, their presence began to impinge upon his OCPD world. By then, however, he had no separate residence to escape to. He was forced to deal with the problems and disarray of the real world. The pressure mounted rapidly. Then one day Kevin discovered that his wife had committed a cardinal sin against someone with OCPD: Rachel, who wasn't even "allowed" access to their money, had overdrawn the checking account.

His sexual addiction had already reached an all-time deprivation point, and his displaced anger was raging. Kevin blew. He stripped naked, tied Rachel up, gagged her, pulled her pants down, and beat her with a belt until he reached a sexual climax. The episode mirrored the porn he had been involved with for so many years. Afterward, Kevin was relaxed and calm.

Following that incident and after much counseling, Rachel divorced him.

There are many more stories about family and friends who have been shocked by the secret sex life of someone with OCPD. They're unaware that the oh-so-clean and mechanized world of their loved one comes with a dirty secret release valve. My wife clearly remembers her father keeping pornographic magazines, even as he held everyone and everything else to the highest of standards.

If someone you're living with shows signs of OCPD, they may also have hidden sexual perversions. You, however, do not have to stay stuck with the guilt and shame of OCPD and deviant sexual behavior.

Chapter 9

Paranoid Personality Disorder

I ndividuals with paranoid personality disorder have a pervasive distrust and suspiciousness of others, often interpreting their motives as malevolent. It usually begins by early adulthood, and the DSM states that it is indicated by four or more of the following:

- Suspicion, without sufficient basis, that others are exploiting, harming or deceiving them.

- Preoccupation with unjustified doubts about the loyalty or trustworthiness of friends or associates.

- Reluctance to confide in others because of unwarranted fear that the information will be used maliciously against them.

- Reading hidden demeaning or threatening meanings into benign remarks or events.

- Persistently harboring grudges, i.e., unforgiving of insults, injuries or slights.

- Perceiving attacks on their character or reputation that are not apparent to others; quick to react angrily or to counterattack.

- Holding recurrent suspicions, without justification, about the fidelity of spouse or sexual partner.

James and Betty's Story

It was late one night after my radio broadcast when I got the call from James, a 49-year-old chemical engineer who worked for a major space production company. He said he was driving home from work when he caught my radio show about anger. James said he had been very angry for a long time and wanted to do something about it. When he arrived at my office the next day, I was greeted by a man who was very polite and cordial, and I had trouble imagining that such a nice person could have an anger problem.

As he told me his story, I saw a pattern. He said he needed me to help him learn how to deal with his wife, who continued to side with her siblings and friends against him.

I said, "James, that sounds like a legitimate beef. I would feel a bit angry if my wife took everyone's side but mine. Let me meet with your wife so I can find out why she would do such a thing."

He looked at me with a blank stare. I asked, "What's wrong, Jim?"

He replied, "You know, we've been to a bunch of counselors, and she convinced them all that I'm the problem."

As a counselor, my antenna goes up every time someone claims they have been to many counselors with no resolution. It is a big red flag when a person goes from one professional to another, never finding the answer they want.

I convinced James to trust me, and the next day I got a call from James' wife, Betty. She also was very cooperative, and it seemed as if she had done this before. Betty was an elementary school teacher. She and James had been married for 23 years and had raised four children together.

I asked Betty about their experience with other counselors and what she thought about her husband's allegations. As we spoke, it became obvious that she wasn't as mean and conniving as James had portrayed her. Betty said that about 10 years before, after James made a major career change, he had started accusing her of disrespecting and betraying him. The more she gave to James, agreed with him, and pampered him, the worse the situation became. James accused her siblings of making fun of him in front of their children during family get-togethers. He accused her parents of disliking him.

Betty said her parents had always loved James and treated him very well, and it was the same with her siblings. James had become very depressed after a younger engineer at work was advanced to a position similar to his, she said. She then revealed that James' mother had displayed the same behavior toward his father for years. Her mother-in-law, in a panic, would call, saying that James' father was going to kill her with a knife. The children would drop everything and run over to their house, and there James' dad would be, calming his wife and explaining to the children that their mother was just having another "episode." After a while, the children became accustomed to her false alarms.

I told Betty that if the information she was sharing was true, her husband needed to be on medication because it sounded as if he had almost certainly inherited his paranoia from his mother's side of the family.

Betty then looked down and shook her head, saying, "You'll never get him to take medication. He thinks all the drug companies are out to poison us. He doesn't trust doctors, lawyers or psychiatrists."

I asked her: "Who does he trust?"

"No one," she said. "Everyone is a suspect to him, and you will be too now that you've spoken to me. Once anyone talks to me about him, he starts accusing that person of conspiring against him. Everything is because of me."

I was inclined to believe Betty, but it wasn't until James came to his next visit that I saw firsthand exactly what she was talking about.

James said, "You spoke to my wife?"

"Yes, James, I did."

"Well, what did she say?"

"She didn't quite give me the same story you did, but —"

"I knew it," he said, in a voice that was suddenly much more challenging. "I knew if you spoke to her, she would flatter you like she has everyone else. And you fell for it."

"James," I said, "She didn't flatter me at —"

"Why are you accusing me of lying? You have joined her, and now you're going to peg me as the bad guy."

"James!" I said in a voice raised enough to get his attention. "You need medication! It will help you!"

He stood and lectured me about how the big drug companies have brainwashed me to push their profits, and how I was a disciple of a corrupt, capitalistic society.

I no longer had any doubts about why Betty would shut down and move to another bedroom, avoiding her husband at all cost. No matter what she did or didn't do, James would still have the same ideas and opinions about her. James was suffering from paranoid personality disorder and needed medication, which left Betty feeling hopeless and stuck.

People with paranoid personality disorder always have unmet expectations because of the unrealistic fears running through their brains. They believe most people are thwarting them, which causes them to be angry and depressed. Their families are also angry because they assume their loved one is just being an infuriating pain who should soon come to his or her senses. But it never happens. And it never will unless the person with paranoid personality disorder is properly diagnosed and medicated. Hopefully this happens before the condition passes the point of no return.

James never agreed to get medical help, and Betty finally filed for divorce.

If you're wondering why you can't break through to someone who is constantly suspicious of you and almost everyone else, then you are most likely dealing with a serious paranoid disorder. This could be why you are staying stuck.

Chapter 10

Narcissistic
Personality Disorder

I n Greek mythology, Narcissus was a handsome youth who rejected the desperate advances of the nymph Echo. As punishment, he was cursed to fall in love with his own reflection in a pool of water. Unable to consummate his love, Narcissus pined away and changed into the flower that bears his name.

And so it is with those diagnosed with narcissistic personality disorder. The person is consumed with themselves and believes that the world revolves around them, and them alone. According to the diagnostic criteria from the DSM, at least five of the following are necessary for a diagnosis of narcissism:

- A grandiose sense of self-importance.

- Preoccupation with fantasies of unlimited success,

power, brilliance, beauty or ideal love.

- Belief that they are special and unique, and can only be understood by other special people.

- Need for excessive admiration.

- Strong sense of entitlement.

- Tendency to take advantage of others to achieve their own ends.

- Lack of empathy.

- Often envious or believe that others are envious of them.

- Arrogant demeanor.

Jane's Story

I had just finished speaking to a group of single adults about anger and depression when a woman from the audience approached me. Her name was Jane, and she was embroiled in a battle to get primary custody of her three small children. For the last two years, Jane had been fighting a judge's decision that had ordered her to share custody equally with her ex-husband. She had lost court case after court case.

I have never seen 50-50 custody arrangements work successfully. Some family courts seem to look at parenting through a politically correct View-Master that causes them to think such an arrangement can work, but we in the behavioral profession can never compromise the mental and emotional health of children for such a seemingly easy fix.

While some courts are stricken with the "no-fault parent" syndrome, I and many other professionals believe primary custody must always go to the more stable parent. On more than one occasion I have seen family courts take the side of social workers who themselves had never been married, with no children of their own, and with no understanding of destructive human behavior. Children caught in split parenting become confused about which parent is right and which is wrong; moreover, it gives dysfunctional parents the opportunity to use their children as tools to inflict pain on the innocent parent.

I asked Jane, "How did this happen? Usually the more responsible parent gets primary custodial care while the other gets visitation, and usually it's the woman who gets the favorable judgment."

Jane started to cry. "I've been hearing that question for the entire two years I've been in litigation," she said, and then explained, "The court said I was too out-of-control to have the children full-time after I lost it once while testifying. I was on the stand, and my ex's lawyer was once again lying about me and my children. He goaded and manipulated me until I just lost it."

Also working against her was how slick and charming her ex-husband, Fred, was with his convincing tales about "crazy" Jane.

Fred was an insurance salesman who first met Jane at a sales convention. He was good-looking and very persuasive, and Jane fell for him hook, line and sinker. She thought Fred would be not only fun and attentive, but also a very successful provider. The couple wed about six months after their first romantic encounter, right before the death of Jane's dad. She said Fred immediately swooped in like a bird of prey, playing the concerned son-in-law to her widowed mother, who was wealthy. He convinced Jane's mother to reinvest the accounts that Jane's father had left her and to change the life insurance policies over to something "more affordable." He also used her inheritance money to buy properties in his name alone.

When at first Jane's mother was skeptical, Fred convinced Jane to talk her mother into the changes by telling her it was for the family's long-term stability. As for Jane, she trusted her husband and was eager to do anything that would bring about a good future for her marriage and her family.

Fred continued to convince Jane and her mother to sign for large loans, insurance policies and mortgages. After 10 years, Jane's finances were looking very grim. Finally Jane became concerned that Fred's "investments" were not producing and started questioning his practices. When she refused to cooperate with Fred until she got a full accounting of the money, he punished her verbally and emotionally, calling her names and degrading her character. He told her she was unattractive and would never be able to make it without him.

The reason he avoided her questions about the money was because he was collecting large payouts from the insurance policies and loans and hiding them. Huge amounts of cash were nowhere to be found. Meanwhile, Fred never made one payment on the loans because they were not in his name. He knew he could collect the cash, never pay the loan back, and stick Jane and her mother for the debt.

The financial games and the verbal abuse continued, but it wasn't until Jane found out that Fred had been committing adultery the whole time they had been married that she filed for divorce. This enraged Fred even more. A narcissist never likes to feel controlled or overpowered, even if they are in the wrong.

By the time the couple went to court, Jane's attorney was unable to track any of the *more than $500,000* Fred had hidden away. Not only was Jane unable to retrieve the money Fred had stolen from her and her 78-year-old mother, but she ultimately was ordered by the court to pay off the full amount of the loans.

Fred had portrayed Jane and her mother as spendthrifts who racked up the loans feeding their shopping habit. Fred also convinced the court that whenever he told Jane she should stay home and take care of the children instead of shopping, she would fly into a rage. Then Fred's attorney displayed the loan papers with Jane and her mother's signatures. And that's when Jane lost it. Regrettably, when she did, the jury was convinced that the charming ex-husband was telling the truth. They decided Fred didn't have to pay alimony because Jane had plenty of money from the loans. They were sure he would be devastated if he couldn't see his children half the time. Fred of course wanted only to avoid paying child support.

Jane could not believe that someone she shared her life with could do such a thing. She was sick to her stomach to think that she had been taken so badly.

Fred continued to take Jane back to court to use his children to get more money, even though in the 10 years he was married to Jane he never made any on his own. Knowing his own inability to support himself, he wasn't going to stop until he had wrangled every dime possible from Jane's mother.

After the divorce, he invited his girlfriend to move in — so she could watch his children. The money he had accumulated from Jane's family went toward extravagant trips with her and his children, which fit perfectly into his plan to punish Jane while convincing the court he was a good dad.

You see, a narcissist never stops punishing. Nothing satisfies them. Their goal isn't just to use anyone and everyone in order to feed their insatiable hunger for power and control; they also like to watch people squirm under their dictatorial thumb. It is impossible to negotiate or have a reciprocal relationship with a narcissist. The only thing that has ever stopped them is their own destruction. Individuals like

Saddam Hussein, Osama Bin Laden and Adolph Hitler are extreme examples of narcissism, the so-called disorder that has caused more pain and destruction than any personality problem I have ever seen.

At this point, I probably need to clarify something. You must understand that there are many people suffering from personality disorders who also have narcissistic tendencies and yet are not narcissistic in the clinical sense of the word. A true narcissist doesn't have any other mood disorder motivating his or her extreme selfishness.

If you are involved with a narcissist, you likely are living in a constant state of fear, anger and depression. It may seem as if there's no way out of a narcissist's power and control, but there is. You must get the help of a trained counselor. Narcissists are so slick and convincing that they will keep luring you back into their tenacious grip, only to punish you again. Don't fall for it.

If you are stuck with a narcissist, you will never be able to give enough love to see any real change. Get away. Run. And don't look back.

Chapter 11

Addictions
and Self-Medication

An addiction can be a chronic disorder brought on by a combination of genetic, biological, pharmacological, environmental and other factors. It is characterized by the repeated use of a substance or behavior that continues to cause problems in a person's financial, relational and physical health. Addictions can include compulsive behaviors such as drug use, overeating, sex or gambling.

In all cases, the term addiction describes a chronic pattern of behavior that the sufferer perceives is difficult or impossible to quit. It is quite common for an addict to express a desire to stop without being able to.

Another description of addiction is an ongoing escalation in the behavior, followed by withdrawal symptoms in its absence. Drugs and compulsive behaviors that provide either pleasure or relief from pain pose a higher risk of being addictive.

I've heard it said that the definition of an addiction is the absence of pain at all cost. It appears that people who are addicted to a substance or unhealthy repetitive behavior are usually people who will do just about anything to avoid pain.

It's natural for living creatures to avoid pain. Still, some animals have been known to chew their own leg off in order to escape the steel teeth of a trap. In such cases, fear of death far outweighs the pain of losing a limb. But with an addict, death isn't the most feared; pain is. A compulsive gambler gambles to remove the pain of an everyday disappointment, and so it is with sex addicts, obsessive-compulsive hand washers, overeaters, and most other addicts. They're all trying to ease a pain from the past, from the present, from the future — or all three. While it's natural for us to take the path of least resistance, the one we ultimately choose — either the wide, easy one that leads to addictions or the narrow, difficult one that leads to success — is determined from early childhood.

There is a desperate, innate drive in humans to seek out the Garden of Eden. When a person's ultimate goal is to feel pleasure and to have no opposition in life, they will seek out an anesthetic from the stark truth that they may have to work through pain, disappointment and rejection in order to find true success and fulfillment. This desire to numb the pain causes addictive people to end up with every struggle they thought they were escaping. This is why it's vital for parents to help children understand that anything good and pleasurable comes with a price. Teens must understand that rejection from close friends, breakups with boyfriends and girlfriends, and scoldings from coaches, teachers and bosses are normal conflicts in this big world. They must also understand there is a price to pay for everything that is good in life.

My wife and I understand the struggle of parenting teens, especially when it comes to teaching them not to take the path of least resistance. Proper and responsible parenting always requires adolescents to begin adapting to the fact that life is no bed of roses.

Vicki and I have a motto with our children: We do not reward poor and irresponsible choices that lead to what children would like to call "mistakes." If they choose to follow the wrong crowd, have a wild party at college, or get involved in a questionable relationship, we allow the prodigal child, for his or her own sake, to suffer reasonable consequences. If they're in school, getting good grades, and involved in extracurricular activities, we'll go the extra mile for them. We don't mind sacrificing to make sure they have a car, gas, clothes and fun if they are doing what they are supposed to.

But too many parents reward poor behavior by bailing their children out of sticky situations they have willfully chosen to involve themselves in. These unlucky young people quickly become accustomed to mom and dad removing consequences, and they become conditioned to think that there are easier ways to get through life. Children who always get rescued will eventually get old enough to be held responsible for their actions by an authority larger than mom or dad. By this time, choosing the path of least resistance will fail them, and they will be crippled in their ability to recover.

Many adult children who cannot keep a job, stay faithful to their spouse, or take responsibility for their children are adults who have developed an addictive personality disorder. They just do not believe they should have to put much effort into anything they don't want to. Parents who feed this type of escapism are parents who do not want the pain and struggle of disciplining their offspring themselves. These parents are exhibiting an addiction of their own.

Rhonda's Story

Rhonda was coming to me for counseling because of her struggles with relationships and family. On her evaluation questionnaire she noted that she and her younger brother were adopted. Even though Rhonda was in her mid-40s, she was still tied financially to her parents. After working with Rhonda for a while, she was able to accept the fact that many of her struggles with relationships and career choices stemmed from the fact that her parents continued to bail her out of any predicament she got herself into.

It appeared that Rhonda was functioning at a low-level addictive attitude, something that happens quite often with adopted children. Parents who were unable to conceive often are so elated to have a child in their life that they become over-protective parents.

According to Rhonda, she wasn't affected nearly as bad as her brother, who was two years younger. Rhonda said that back in junior high Leonard had started taking drugs, and when he was kicked out of school for smoking pot, her parents blamed the school. At age 19, Leonard got his girl-friend pregnant. Of course mom and dad financially supported all three of them.

The more addicted Leonard became, the more Rhonda's parents pampered him. Leonard knew from an early age that taking the path of least resistance paid off. He didn't have to do anything he didn't like, and he would just smoke a joint or drink a beer if he felt too much pressure. Mom and dad would continue to take care of him.

At age 42, brother Leonard was living at home with his parents, now in their late 70s. After three divorces and two children, Leonard was without a job, addicted to alcohol, pot and cigarettes, and in poor health from his lifestyle. And Rhonda's parents were still footing the bill. It should be noted that, because of Leonard's addiction, he might have had a chemical imbalance, as I mentioned in an earlier chapter.

But whether an addiction is induced by a chemical imbalance or the way a person was raised, it still needs to be confronted and stopped. The only way Leonard would ever have a chance to recover would be if Rhonda's parents decided to risk Leonard's pain and rejection and put a stop to their enabling. In most cases of adult child dependency, the elderly parents usually go to their graves feeling guilty and responsible for the addicted offspring.

Brother Marty

My older brother Marty served two years in Vietnam, and when he returned home in 1969, we were so thrilled to see him. I was 12 years old at that time, sandwiched between three other brothers who were either a few years younger or older. Because of the age gap between the youngest brothers and Marty, we looked to him more as a father figure than we did our own aging dad.

Soon after Marty returned from Vietnam, he joined the Detroit police department. There he got a terrifying look at what illegal drugs did to those who used them, and it affected him profoundly. So much so that one day Marty, in his tough, cop-like way, decided to teach us younger brothers about drugs.

It was during one of his usual visits to see my parents that he told us boys to take a walk with him in the woods behind our 2-acre plot. After following him to the back of the property where no one could see us, he stopped, reached behind him, and pulled a .357 police revolver from his belt. Wow! I thought that, at age 14, I was about to shoot a gun. But that wasn't what Marty had in mind at all.

He held the pistol out and, pointed it into the ground, and said "See this gun?" We nodded that we did indeed see it.

"If any of you ever touch drugs," Marty said quietly, "I will take you back here where Mom can't see or hear us, and I'll put you out of your misery."

Our knees were shaking and our eyes were wide with fear as my brother continued, "Once you start taking street drugs, there is no hope for you. I've seen what happens to kids once they start down that path. They kill their parents, lie, cheat and steal to get their fix. I have decided you would be better off dead than living like that."

After this short — but effective — dissertation, he tucked the revolver back in his belt, and said, "OK. Let's go back up to the house and have some fun."

It was years before we told Mom what Marty did. In the meantime, none of my four brothers ever touched drugs, even when most of our friends in the '70s were doing it.

As a professional counselor, I cannot recommend that tactic. But I have to say that the Marty Joseph Show-and-Tell School of Drug Prevention effectively saved me. I thank my brother for caring enough to save my life from addictions. And, years later, when it came time for me to deal with my own son, I remembered Marty's tough method.

We must take drug addiction very seriously — to the point of sacrificing our own reputation — in order to save the next generation. If we don't, all the mushy, gushy love in the world will never be enough to avoid staying stuck in our recovery.

Self-Medicating

When an addicted person comes to me for counseling, I always question them about their drug of choice. Some like cigarettes, others cocaine. One prefers pot, while another chooses alcohol. Individuals gravitate toward particular substances based on what they're longing for. When I listen closely enough, the addict tells me a story.

My experience is that self-medicating is a clear indication that the person is someone who longs to feel good. As a clinical counselor, I had to learn that those who are struggling with a substance abuse problem are desperately trying to fix a real chemical imbalance in their body. Many times I've referred someone with a persistent addiction to a physician who was able to prescribe a medication that completed their chemistry.

While there have been times when I myself wanted to feel better or escape the world's cares for a while, I'm fortunate enough not to have a genetic predisposition to addictions. There are many others, however, who cannot imbibe any potentially addictive substance without their physical chemistry demanding to experience that good feeling once more. It's not unusual then, as I mentioned earlier, for someone who is depressed because of a chemical imbalance to seek out an addictive substance to relieve their pain.

Laura's Story

Laura was a middle-aged woman who needed help with her new husband, Sam, and his alcohol problem. Drinking had already cost Sam his first marriage, and it was well on its way to costing him his marriage to Laura.

As for Laura, she was a typical codependent rescuer and had bailed Sam out of his legal bills even before she walked down the aisle and said, "I do." While her enabling behavior played a major role in their marriage problems, Sam was the one who had to stop drinking before we could deal with Laura's issues. The couple was in debt because of his DUIs, legal fees and hospital bills, all related to alcohol abuse. You would think that someone who had lost everything once before to alcohol and was on the verge of doing so again would finally get it, but those of us who are not of the same genetic constitution as the addict will never understand what they really feel.

Because Sam was very much in love with Laura and afraid of losing her, he was willing to do anything to save his marriage. I asked him if he had ever had medical and psychiatric evaluations to find out if he was depressed or had a chemical imbalance. It turned out that, despite all his many troubles related to alcohol, no one had ever before suggested that he be evaluated.

I asked Sam to see his family physician and relate his history of drinking, along with the fact that I suggested he be evaluated for depression. Sam obediently did as I suggested. As I had hoped, his doctor put him on an antidepressant known to achieve what Sam was trying to get from alcohol. After 30 days of taking the medication, Sam stopped drinking. His marriage improved and he did not relapse, even when he was under pressure. The new prescription had helped balance Sam's chemistry so that his body didn't cry out for alcohol.

When someone's addiction is not for a depressant such as alcohol but to something like cocaine, "meth," or an amphetamine, this tells me that this person craves stimulation. This addiction would require a much different approach because their body is crying out for more energy.

Even though taking a prescription medication is not the answer for all who suffer with an addiction, I still say that a person should to seek out professional help to learn what their body is craving before staying stuck by self-medicating.

Chapter 12

Sins of the Fathers: Generational Dysfunctions

The year was 1900. The place, Elllis Island, New York. My grandparents and several other members of the family had emigrated from the northern mountains of Lebanon to escape persecution by Muslim Lebanese. My grandparents were Christians and, according to the fundamental Muslims, were to be exterminated.

My great aunt Maggie settled in Toledo, OH, where she raised nine children. She gave birth to her fifth child in 1912 on a hay wagon. They named him Amos. Her brother and sister-in-law were not able to conceive a child, and so Aunt Maggie graciously gave Amos to them to raise. Aunt Maggie eventually had four more children.

As little Amos grew, he would play with his siblings down the street, thinking they were his cousins. He was raised quite differently from them. While they were fighting for food, sharing beds, and getting very little attention because their mother was too busy and their father was an alcoholic and a gambler, Amos was given plenty of attention, lots of positive reinforcement, and was trained to mind his manners.

By the time he was an adolescent, Amos had learned the truth that his cousins were actually his siblings, and he grew very close to his brothers. Around the time of the Great Depression, he and his older brother Ray decided they would make some money by selling the *Toledo Blade* newspaper on street corners and by selling candy at a burlesque show.

As Amos and Ray watched the entertainers perform, they began to dream of becoming singers, dancers and comedians like those they saw on the stage. So they started performing on the streets of Toledo and found that they were indeed good enough to make a few bucks entertaining others.

From the stories my parents told, Amos was not quite as talented as Ray. But when Ray was nearly 20, he started dating a young lady who wanted him to give up the silly notion of becoming an entertainer and get a real job that would allow them to get married and raise a family. So Ray quit showbiz, got married, and became a house painter. But Amos refused to succumb to defeat and found ways to travel the 60 miles to Detroit for gigs on the radio and in nightclubs, all the while dreaming he might someday be "discovered."

One day while at a radio show in Detroit, he met a beautiful Italian woman named Rose Marie. They soon wed. After the birth of their first child, Rose Marie went to live with Aunt Maggie in Toledo while Amos headed for Cleveland to give showbiz one last shot.

Years later, Uncle Amos himself told me about that trip. He was headed for a nightclub in Cleveland when he suddenly felt compelled to turn west and go instead to Chicago. Once there, he prayed to the patron saint of desperate cases and lost causes, Saint Jude. He promised God that if he made it big he would find a way to help children with serious illnesses. You see, when Amos was younger, his little brother was bitten by a rat and almost died because Aunt Maggie couldn't afford proper medical treatment.

Amos eventually found a place to work as an emcee in a big Chicago nightclub called the 5100 Club. Worried that he would flop and ruin his good name, he took an alias: Danny, which was his younger brother's name, and Thomas, from his older brother. Uncle Amos, better known as Danny Thomas, then began a career that would lead him to become one of America's greatest and most beloved entertainers and movie producers in TV history.

In the 1950s and '60s he starred in the comedies "Make Room For Daddy" and "The Danny Thomas Show." He also was the executive producer for television classics such as "The Andy Griffith Show," "Gomer Pyle, U.S.M.C.," "The Real McCoys," and "The Dick Van Dyke Show." But his greatest achievement was founding St. Jude Children's Research Hospital, known worldwide for its treatment of children with catastrophic illnesses.

So why am I telling you this story? Because most of Danny Thomas' brothers, who were raised so differently than he, became alcoholics, gamblers and womanizers like their father, while Amos mimicked the resilient, hard-working parents with whom he lived. Family influence plays a huge role in the way people process conflict and resolutions, make decisions, and develop relationships. One of the songs Danny Thomas sings in the 1952 version of the motion picture "The Jazz Singer" is a perfect reflection of the choice he had to make when it came to giving up his dream. As I remember, one line says, "I'm living the life I love, and I'm loving the life I live." Ideally, every adult should be able to sing that same song; whether or not they will depends largely upon how they were raised.

Pavlov's theory of conditioned response demonstrates how parenting affects a person's life. Most of us know about the experiments that Ivan Pavlov (1849-1936) conducted with a dog and a bell. He rang a bell as the dog was fed until, after a while, the dog would salivate at the mere sound of the bell.

In the same way, people are conditioned by their parents to respond based on punishment and reward. When we look at the Middle East crisis, we see a prime example of conditioned response. Children in this region are taught from birth that their way of life is the only way to truth and that western-ized living is to be hated. Even when offered demonstrable proof that the United States is a decent place with good people, they still believe the illusion taught them by their forefathers. Generation after generation of negative parental influence has established destructive patterns for entire peoples.

In the same way, cycles of addictions and abuse continue in families that view the world solely through the eyes of their dysfunctional forefathers. It still amazes me how many of my patients say their problems show up throughout their family tree.

I once heard a story about a circus bear that was kept in a 12- by 12-foot cage from the time it was a wee cub. For 11 years, he paced 12 feet forward and 12 feet back. Sometimes visitors threw food and drinks at him, and the bear would stop momentarily and eat whatever was thrown his way before returning to his pacing.

When his owner died, he was donated to a zoo that prided itself on arranging natural habitats for its animals. The bear enclosure there was a beautiful sanctuary with rolling hills, green trees and refreshing ponds.

When the bear was moved in his old cage to the new place, he ran to the back of the cage and stubbornly refused to exit. They literally had to light a fire under him, using a torch to force him outdoors into the habitat. When his large body tumbled onto the lush, green grass, the bear looked around with confusion, then ran about 20 feet. He stopped, walked 12 feet forward, then 12 feet back. When it finally became clear that the bear's conditioned upbringing would not allow him to adapt to his new, and much improved, circumstances, zookeepers euthanized him.

It is vital that those who are seeking recovery understand that their own family could be keeping them stuck. Being confined by abuse can become habitual. Even when freedom through counseling and treatment is available, some refuse to accept it because a world without the dysfunctional dynamics to which they've become accustomed seems too unfamiliar and frightening. In such cases, victims must retrain their thinking, or recondition themselves, in order to recover from the sins of their forefathers.

The truth is, just because someone holds the title of parent, spouse, brother, sister, boss or pastor, doesn't mean they qualify as God. My oldest stepdaughter once gave me a decorative throw pillow for my office that says, "Any man can be a father, but it takes someone special to be a dad." That says it all.

Unless it is removed, generational dysfunction will always override love, freedom, and common sense and is yet another reason why many stay stuck in their emotional, relational and behavioral healing.

So how do you break the cycle? In the following pages, you'll see 1) how to break negative conditioned responses, 2) the signs of a dysfunctional home, and 3) some of the biggest reasons we avoid confronting family members.

Top 10 Ways to Break
Negative Conditioned Responses

Accept the fact that:

• All learned behavior should be questioned.

• Your parents (and all adult figures) are not, and never were, God.

• Truth should be measured, not by your perception of it, but by its long-term outcome.

• When you break with tradition, rejection from close family and friends is likely.

• During your reconditioning, expect to be uncomfortable.

• Pain is part of recovery.

• Failure is a part of life and certainly to be expected during any recovery.

• When you cast off an old family belief system, you'll have to grieve for it as you would any loss.

• We can be so sentimental for the familiar that we never move ahead.

• You will need the encouragement of a support group and/or counselor to sustain you.

Ten Characteristics
Of a Dysfunctional Home Life

1. Incest of any kind — either physical or emotional.

2. Abuse of any kind — slapping, hitting, punching, condemning, etc.

3. After the age of comprehension, seeing your opposite-sex parent naked.

4. Witnessing your parents having sex.

5. Seeing your parents supply alcohol to a minor or they themselves drinking to get drunk.

6. Knowing your parents are involved in substance abuse.

7. Exposure to smoking by your parents.

8. Exposure to explicit language and/or images by parents or siblings.

9. Feeling that you had to protect your parents' feelings of depression or despair.

10. An overly strict, religious environment where everything is a "sin."

Top 10 Reasons
We Don't Confront an Abusive Family Member

1. We fear the reaction of family members.

2. We feel the need to protect family members just because they're family.

3. We're afraid of being rejected by family members.

4. We're embarrassed and ashamed about the incident(s).

5. It's easier to blame ourselves than to confront the abusive person.

6. We misinterpret the Christian teaching to honor our father and mother.

7. Our reluctance to give up family ties.

8. We think we somehow elicited the abuse.

9. We don't know how to go about confronting the person.

10. We don't have the support we need.

In the top photo, my mother and father are on the left with Dad's cousin, Amos, aka Danny Thomas, right after I was born in 1957. Below that, Amos is pictured with my two older brothers, Marty (on the left) and Bill (on the right), while they were stationed in California during the Vietnam War. At left, I am pictured with Uncle Amos in 1981, when I was attending college in Grand Rapids, MI. He was performing there at the Amway Grand Plaza Hotel.

Chapter 13

Inborn Temperaments

D iscussion of inborn temperament is nothing new. According to *Creation therapy: A Biblically based model for Christian counseling* by Drs. Richard and Phyllis Arno, Hippocrates (460-370 BC) was the first to bring the theory to light, and even he may have been building on the thoughts of Empedocles (490-430 BC).

According to Hippocrates, behavior was governed by certain body fluids that he called "humors." The fluids were blood, black bile, yellow bile and phlegm. He believed that an excess of one humor would cause the person to have certain tendencies; e.g., someone with an overabundance of black bile would be dark and moody person, as in the melancholy temperament.

While Hippocrates' humors may not have held up scientifically, they were the genesis of some basic understanding about the differences in human behavior.

In 1927 Alfred Adler interpreted Hippocrates' four temperaments into the sanguine, choleric, melancholy and phlegmatic. Adler believed sanguines were the healthiest type because they were not subject to severe deprivations and humiliation, had very few feelings of inferiority, and strived for superiority in a happy, friendly manner.

He saw the choleric temperament as very aggressive and intense, always striving to be on top, and willing to expend great amounts of energy to get there. He described melancholy types as those who felt inferior, were worriers, and lacked the discipline and initiative to make decisions when risks were involved. Although the melancholy type was not especially antisocial, they generally chose not to associate. Phlegmatics, he said, were depressed, slow and sluggish and had lost contact with life.

Hans J. Eysenck (1916-1997) was a well-known German psychologist who added to the theory of temperaments with his research in which he analyzed personality differences using a psychostatistical method. Eysenck's research led him to believe that temperament is biologically based.

In 1984, the National Christian Counselors Association identified a fifth inborn temperament type called the supine, which we touched on in Chapter 7 while dealing with dependency disorder.

The NCCA also developed a clinical test to ascertain temperament types, information that is invaluable to both the counselor and the one being counseled. According to the

NCCA, people display one of the five temperament types in three different areas.

The areas are:

- **Inclusion** (the mind), which deals with the way we socialize and the way our mind operates.

- **Control** (the will), which deals with how we control and are controlled and with how we make decisions.

- **Affection** (our emotions), which deals with how we give and receive love, approval and affection.

This means, for instance, that someone could be melancholy in the area of inclusion, choleric in the area of control, and sanguine in the area of affection.

Temperament testing is useful for:

- understanding your spouse and children,

- finding the career that is most comfortable for you,

- finding hobbies and relationships that will bring you the most satisfaction,

- determining how you make decisions and take on responsibilities,

- identifying how dependent or independent you are,

- helping you feel comfortable about who you are, and

- learning how you understand and help those with whom you live and work.

On the following pages, you'll find a breakdown of the strengths and weaknesses of the five temperament types in each of the three areas of inclusion, control and affection.

CHOLERIC

Inclusion strengths	Control strengths	Affection strengths
Open, friendly, confident, outgoing, optimistic	Very strong-willed	Open, optimistic and outgoing
Tough-minded	Very good leadership abilities	Capable of giving a great deal of love and affection
Perfectionist	Capable of making intuitive decisions	Selective about deep relationships
Good at envisioning new projects	Capable of taking on responsibilities	**Affection weaknesses**
Inclusion weaknesses	Has a "no giving up" attitude	Indirect behavior
Hot temper	**Control weaknesses**	Can reject others' love after getting what they need
Can be a people user	Angry, impatient, cruel	Can reject loving people
Can be angry and cruel	Can adopt very bad behavior in order to keep control	Can be cruel to those who reject them
	Will associate with weak people in order to dominate them, then resent them for being weak	

SANGUINE

Inclusion strengths

Very friendly, outgoing, inspiring, enthusiastic, warm, optimistic

Relationship-oriented

Sees the bright side of things

Loves people and socializing

Freely interacts with all types of people

Inclusion weaknesses

Can be too talkative

Wants to be the center of attention

Can adopt bad behaviors and morals to avoid rejection

Impulsive

Undisciplined

Prone to exaggerate

Needs to appear successful

Will ignore responsibilities to socialize and be with people

Control strengths & weaknesses

Swings like a pendulum

Can be very independent, responsible, controlling, and aggressive, then swing to self-indulgent, dependent, and irresponsible. The changes can be either positive or negative.

Affection strengths

Express large amounts of love and affection

Warm

Emotionally open

Affection weaknesses

Easily devastated if not reassured they are loved and appreciated

Can be very demanding for others to love them

Can adopt poor behaviors to get the love they feel they need

SUPINE

Inclusion strengths

Capacity to serve others

Loving

Gentle spirit

Inclusion weaknesses

Indirect behavior
(expects others to read
their mind)

Fear of rejection

Control strengths

Very dependable

Very giving and
service-oriented

Rule-keeper

Very loyal

Control weaknesses

Gets hurt easily

Non-aggressive

Very dependent on
others to make
decisions

Difficulty saying "no"

Usually feels
powerless and at the
mercy of others

Believes everyone

Affection strengths

Ability to respond to
love

Very open to sharing
emotions with safe
people

Committed to deep
relationships

Affection weaknesses

Inability to initiate love
and affection

Always need reassur-
ance they are loved
even after telling them
yesterday

Covers anger by being
"hurt"

PHLEGMATIC

Inclusion strengths

Ability to perform tedious tasks

Relates both to people and tasks

Calm, easygoing, and extremely efficient

Inclusion weaknesses

Unwillingness to become involved

Observer rather than a participant

Can be very sarcastic

Control strengths

Very practical, conservative, peace-loving

Good arbitrator (wants peace and calm)

Control weaknesses

Indecisive

Can procrastinate

Stubborn

Very difficult to motivate

Affection strength

Well-balanced, calm, with realistic demands for love and affection

Affection weaknesses

Unwillingness to become involved in deep relationships

Tends to be an observer only, unemotional

Rarely self-sacrificing

Inexpressive

MELANCHOLY

Inclusion strengths

Introvert

Loner

Great thinker

Genius-prone

Artistic and creative

Critical, challenging mind

Great understanding of tasks and systems

Perfectionist and self-willed

Inclusion weaknesses

Moody

Prone to depression

Pessimistic

Relives the past (thinks too much)

Low self-image

Can reject people

Lack of social initiative

Control strengths

Good decision-making skills

Highly independent

Strong-willed

Good leadership abilities

Control weaknesses

Ridged and inflexible

Fear of failure

Fear of the unknown

Apt to rebel if pushed

Procrastination

Affection strengths

Very faithful, honest

Loyal to friends and coworkers

Self-sacrificing

Affection weaknesses

Can be angry, cruel, vengeful, emotional

Rarely will express how they feel

Can have a low self-image

Can be very sensitive

I have found that administering the temperament test helps counselees understand why they do and feel some of the things they do. Once they understand their basic inborn temperaments, they generally are better able to cope with difficulties past and present. Married couples in particular, once they understand one another's temperaments, tend to have much more patience, compassion and understanding with each other.

The biggest issue in which I see families stuck is with parents who don't understand their child's inborn temperaments. Once a parent sees the printout outlining their child's temperaments, they have clear direction for how to handle that son or daughter in a way that would be fulfilling to them.

If you're stuck in a situation with a loved one, I strongly recommend you consider their temperament types.

Chapter 14

Inductive and Deductive Reasoning

As we have seen with inborn temperaments, so it is with cognitive reasoning. Couples need to understand their partner's perceptions and thought processes in order to communicate effectively.

Communication is much more than speaking the same language; it is understanding how your mate views what is being said. This is where inductive and deductive reasoning come into play.

To put it simply, inductive thinkers start at the bottom and work their way up, while deductive thinkers start at the top and work their way down.

Inductive thinkers cannot understand how deductive thinkers ever get anything done because they always seem to get big ideas but never take the steps to bring them to fruition. In the same way, the deductive thinker wonders how in the world the inductive thinker accomplishes anything substantive because they are so anal about details.

Just think what would happen if two deductive thinkers got together. Both would be looking at the big picture and the results, but no one would take even the smallest of steps to get there. And just imagine what it would be like for two inductive thinkers to be a couple or business partners. They would be so focused on details that goals and accomplishments would always be on hold. There have been many couples who deliberately sought out someone who thought just like them in order to avoid conflicts, only to find out later what a mistake it was.

Of course there can also be problems between inductive and deductive thinkers, particularly when one spouse tries to make the other conform to their way of thinking. When one spouse continues to correct the other because they are "doing it wrong," there is sure to be conflict and confusion about what is really "wrong." The ideal would be for inductive and deductive partners to learn to complement one another's cognitive thinking processes without judging.

I remember the perplexed, worried look on my wife's face the day I suggested we remodel our basement. Vicki has always been a steady plodder who completes tasks in a proper, orderly fashion. When her teachers told her to do a project this way or that, she followed their instructions to the letter. But me — I thought doing things in a conventional way was a waste of time. I took shortcuts and did things my own way. Such maverick thinking doesn't fit well with traditional education, and I was never a good student.

I once heard the following: "Give a lazy man a hard job, and he will find an easier way to do it." That describes me to a T. This deductive thinking of mine wasn't always the best. I made a lot of mistakes and many times felt like a failure because of the way I processed information. But my deductive thinking has also allowed me to accomplish a lot of things that others haven't.

So I convinced Vicki that we could finish out the basement ourselves. Of course I had never remodeled a basement before, but because of my controlling inborn temperament and my deductive thinking, I already had it finished in my head. This made my wife very nervous. Vicki couldn't envision the new basement. All she saw was the big, empty cement pit in front of her.

I told her that if we each just did what we needed to, we could get it done. Never mind that I didn't have the first clue about what it was I needed to do. So I called a friend of mine who does basements and asked him to instruct me on how to get started.

Each week my friend would walk me through the next phase of the work, then leave me alone for a few days while I completed it. Vicki cleaned up after me, kept the rest of the house in order, and organized everything I had laying around. Eventually we had one of the best basements we've ever had. I now use it as my counseling office.

I was a deductive thinker ready to tackle a big goal and could imagine the finished product, while my wife and my friend were inductive thinkers who could take care of all the details to get us there. In the same way, Vicki takes care of the day-to-day details of scheduling, paying the bills, and running my office, while I think up new goals and ideas to help people.

If you're stuck in your relational healing, I highly suggest you consider whether your loved one is an inductive or deductive thinker. Identifying that one characteristic could solve most of your conflicts.

Chapter 15

Money Problems

There is a false assumption that most marital problems stem from money problems. While it's true that most of the couples I counsel blame money for keeping their relationship stuck, I truly believe it's the other way around: Money problems stem from marriage problems.

In the United States' free enterprise system, money problems are most likely behavioral and relational issues. If we were healed mentally and emotionally, we would be healed relationally. And if we were healed relationally, we would be healed financially. And if our finances were healed, our marriages would follow suit.

As we've seen in previous chapters, many of the dysfunctions that kept relationships and individuals stuck have also caused financial struggles. Carelessness with money is a definite symptom of a deeper behavioral issue. I operate my counseling practice as a nonprofit organization; therefore, my clients are not required to pay for counseling. But I do ask them to make a donation because I have found that those who did not invest financially in counseling never follow through with needed changes. Those who are unwilling to invest their money are unwilling to invest themselves. As Matthew 6:21 says, "For where your treasure is, there will your heart be also."

Married couples who are unable share their finances will also be unable to share their hearts. My wife and I suffered financially after blending a family of five children with little to no help from our former spouses. Because Vicki and I stayed in a bad marriage for so long, we were set back that much more. I do want to say that it's amazing how effectively two healthy, goal-oriented people can stretch a budget and recover financially. But couples with relationship issues will always suffer in the pocketbook.

The following news article by Ellen Goodstein and excerpted from Bankrate.com describes lottery winners who ended up broke, primarily because of codependencies and bad habits they had not resolved before they had the "misfortune" of winning a lot of money.

Unlucky lottery winners
who lost their money

Is winning the lottery really a lucky event? Not if you lose the money, say experts and those who fleetingly had it all.

Winning the lottery isn't always what it's cracked up to be," says Evelyn Adams, who won the New Jersey lottery not just once but twice (1985, 1986) to the tune of $5.4 million. Today, the money is gone and Adams lives in a trailer.

"I won the American dream but I lost it, too. It was a very hard fall. It's called rock bottom," says Adams. "Everybody wanted my money. Everybody had their hand out. I never learned one simple word in the English language — 'No.' I wish I had the chance to do it all over again. I'd be much smarter about it now," says Adams, who also lost money at the slot machines in Atlantic City.

"I was a big-time gambler," admits Adams. "I didn't drop a million dollars, but it was a lot of money. I made mistakes, some I regret, some I don't. I'm human. I can't go back now so I just go forward, one step at a time."

Deeper in debt

Suzanne Mullins won $4.2 million in the Virginia lottery in 1993. Now she's deeply in debt to a company that lent her money using the winnings as collateral.

She borrowed $197,746.15, which she agreed to pay back with her yearly checks from the Virginia lottery through 2006. When the rules changed, allowing her to collect her winnings in a lump sum, she cashed out the remaining amount — but stopped making payments on the loan.

She blamed the debt on the lengthy illness of her uninsured son-in-law, who needed $1 million for medical bills.

Mark Kidd, the Roanoke, Va., lawyer who represented the Singer Asset Finance Company who sued Mullins, confirms. He won a judgment for the company against Mullins for $154,147 last May, but they have yet to collect a nickel.

"My understanding is she has no assets," says Kidd.

Back to the basics

Ken Proxmire was a machinist when he won $1 million in the Michigan lottery. He moved to California, went into the car business with his brothers and within five years, Ken had filed for bankruptcy.

"He was just a poor boy who got lucky and wanted to take care of everybody," explains Ken's son Rick. "... There's no more talk of owning a helicopter or riding in limos. We're just everyday folk. Dad's now back to work as a machinist."

Willie Hurt of Lansing, Mich., won $3.1 million in 1989. Two years later, he was broke and charged with murder. His lawyer says Hurt spent his fortune on a divorce and crack cocaine.

Charles Riddle of Belleville, Mich., won $1 million in 1975. Afterward, he got divorced, faced several lawsuits and was indicted for selling cocaine.

Missourian Janite Lee won $18 million in 1993. Lee was generous to a variety of causes, particularly politics, education and the community. But according to published reports, eight years after winning, Lee had filed for bankruptcy with only $700 left in two bank accounts and no cash on hand.

One Southeastern family won $4.2 million in the early '90s. They bought a huge house and succumbed to repeated family requests for help in paying off debts.

The house, cars and relatives used up all their winnings. Eleven years later, the couple is divorcing, the house is sold, and they have to split what is left of the lottery proceeds. The wife got a very small house and the husband has moved in with the kids. Even the life insurance they bought ended up getting cashed in. "It was not the pot of gold at the end of the rainbow," says their financial adviser.

Luck is fleeting

These sad-but-true tales are not uncommon, experts say. "For many people, sudden money can cause disaster," says Susan Bradley, a certified financial planner in Palm Beach, Fla., and founder of the Sudden Money Institute, a resource center for new-money recipients and their advisers.

"In our culture, there is a widely held belief that money solves problems. People think if they had more money, their troubles would be over. When a family receives sudden money, they frequently learn that money can cause as many problems as it solves," she says.

Craig Wallace, a senior funding officer for a company that buys lottery annuity payments in exchange for lump sums, agrees.

"Going broke is a common malady, particularly with the smaller winners. Say you've won $1 million. What you've really won is a promise to be paid $50,000 a year. People win and they think they're millionaires. They go out and buy houses and cars and before they know it, they're in way over their heads," he says.

Are you really a 'millionaire'?

Part of the problem is that the winners buy into the hype.

"These people believe they are millionaires. They buy into the hype, but most of these people will go to their graves without ever becoming a millionaire," says Wallace, who has been in the business for almost a decade.

····

Winning plays a game with your head

Bradley, who wrote "Sudden Money: Managing a Financial Windfall," says winners get into trouble because they fail to address the emotional connection to the windfall.

"There are two sides to money," she says. "The interior side is the psychology of money and the family relationship to money. The exterior side is the tax codes, the money allocation, etc. The goal is to integrate the two. People who can't integrate their interior relationship with money appropriately are more likely to crash and burn.

"Often, they can keep the money and lose family and friends, or lose the money and keep the family and friends — or even lose the money and lose the family and friends."

Alice and Gary's Story

Alice was middle-aged teacher who came for counseling because of the stress related to her family's financial problems. She was a teacher and her husband, Gary, was a developer.

"For years Gary and I would build financial empires, but then, before we knew what hit us, we were broke again," Alice said. "Now I'm in my early fifties and I can't do it anymore." She didn't have health insurance, a savings account, or retirement to lean on, so I asked what her husband was doing to help. She said he was on the verge of another big deal to make millions.

As I probed deeper into the family dynamics, I learned that Gary unwound each night by drinking four or five beers. Her two adult sons had always had problems with Gary because he was too critical, especially after he had drunk a few beers.

I asked Alice, "Do you think your husband has an alcohol problem?"

"I never thought much about it," she answered. "But he does like his beer after a long day."

After I pointed out his pattern of behavior, Alice invited her husband to come for counseling. I had only talked with Gary a short time when it became evident he was an alcoholic with strong bipolar tendencies. It was also clear that he self-medicated with alcohol whenever he was swinging from a manic to a depressed state.

To Alice, Gary was just a hard worker who was able to convince investors to give him lots of money for "large profitable projects," and it was only because of bad luck that the projects eventually fell apart.

The truth was that while Gary was on a manic high, he was able to convince a lot of investors to go in on one "shoe-in" project or another. Once his mania subsided, however, he nosedived into a depression that he medicated with beer.

Alice soon realized that her family's cyclical money problems and bankruptcies were not due to bad karma or a rotten economy, but to a mood disorder and an addiction.

When we pick up on the telltale signs and patterns of behavior that have led to our being stuck in financial problems, we can then address them — and can sometimes repair our money woes in surprisingly short order.

Chapter 16

Living in the Immediate

Just as babies cry to get our attention, so it is with some adults who act out when their physical and emotional needs are not immediately met. When these emotionally underdeveloped adults do not get their way, they throw temper tantrums in front of their spouses, employers and extended family members. They do so because when they were growing up, their real needs were not met —but their temper tantrums elicited an immediate response. Which means they usually got their way.

These grownups are prone to live for the immediate, while those who can project into the future are able to see their needs will eventually be met and so are better able to handle stress and rejection with patience.

As I was watching the History Channel one afternoon, I saw a documentary about primitive cultures and how they had not advanced because they lived only for the immediate.

They did not create long-term plans to develop commerce, inventions and products that would advance their economy. They hunted animals that could be eaten that day. They picked fruit and prepared vegetables that would feed them for one meal at a time. They procreated as their innate drive erupted. They drank water that was available from rain or natural springs. When a drought came and these daily amenities dropped off, so did the people. Their goal and focus went no further than what they needed right then and there, while other cultures developed with foresight and vision. The people of the latter cultures enjoyed prosperity, abundance and better living conditions because they planned.

Benjamin Franklin once said: "By failing to prepare, you are preparing to fail." Our founding forefathers, equipped with centuries of Christian culture and education, immigrated to a land that was occupied by a group of native people who lived largely in the immediate. Even though the Pilgrims had to suffer unspeakable adversity from the elements, illnesses, and uncivilized peoples, they nevertheless were able to take very little and make something of it. One only has to look at the astonishing progress in the United States since that time to appreciate the foresight of the earliest settlers.

I see two obvious things prevalent in a culture that has stopped progressing: immorality and religion, which is different from faith. These two components will cause a nation to live for the immediate more than anything else. Countries like India, Africa and the Middle East are plagued with religion and immorality. They also are plagued with starvation, disease and war.

Our founding fathers, however, left England to get away from a religious society and to establish one based on genuine faith. It's disturbing, then, to see individuals in a civilized, prosperous society like ours living only for the here and now.

But today's instant, get-it-now culture reinforces attitudes that keep us stuck in all areas of life. Overweight people live for the next meal. Sexual deviates live for the next pleasurable moment. Addicts live for their next fix, and alcoholics live for the next drink. Wives cheat on their husbands who have left for work, and husbands cheat while they're at work. Couples run up their credit cards to unimaginable figures. Family members employ a kind of emotional blackmail, making selfish demands in exchange for their love.

When one or more people in a relationship live for immediate gratification rather than a long-term commitment, they will, like any culture, cause their own extinction.

We set up relationships for extinction when we impatiently want our partner to change now, our children to grow up now, our finances to provide independence now, our bodies to lose 20 pounds now. We want a pill to fix something that actually requires a lifestyle change. We demand cures for diseases that could be avoided if we were willing to maintain our health in the first place.

And so it is with behavioral change. We must exercise a long-term, lifetime commitment to recovery. If we are going get unstuck and *stay* unstuck, we must learn to prepare and invest in the future. If counseling would help, seek it out. If medication is needed, see a doctor. If it takes changing your relationships, do it.

Chapter 17

Relapse Relationships

I have attended many seminars and workshops on relapse intervention concerning substance abuse, but there's one relapse intervention seminar I've never seen that a lot of people need. It's a seminar on relapse relationships.

Actually I don't even know if anyone else uses the phrase "relapse relationships," but I had to come up with something to call it after I saw the great many people who continued to reenter destructive relationships. Just like an alcoholic who drinks mouthwash, rubbing alcohol, and even nail polish remover when alcohol is not available, so it is with a person who gets beaten up, kicked around, cheated on, verbally and emotionally abused, and even gets their own children taken away, yet still returns to the cesspool of scum who hurt them.

Perhaps the "repeat defenders" that come to your mind are female, but that is not always the case. Many men also go back again and again to women who have destroyed their lives. Earlier we saw one example in Dale's life. I always wonder: "What goes on in the mind of a victim who continues to relapse toward abusive people? What is the magnet that incessantly attracts them to this type of person?"

The most compelling argument I can come up with to explain this baffling, sick cycle is that some people are so desperate to feel loved and accepted that they won't risk the potential rejection inherent in attempting a new relationship. This need, as we learned earlier regarding low self-esteem, is actually very selfish. When someone's craving to be needed surpasses the dignity and safety of self and/or others, it has become a self-serving behavior. And like I've said, many therapists mistakenly enable these people by pampering their self-pity.

People who are unwilling to give up an abusive relationship need to be strongly challenged. It is important that they see their own selfish behavior in their unwillingness to change.

Many times the pull toward sick relationships indicates depression because someone who is depressed is much more likely to settle for a relationship that gives them instant gratification. This is not love. This is an addictive relationship. Dysfunctional relationships act less like true companionship and more like a sedative. You know you're in a toxic relationship when spending time with them makes you feel as if you have a hangover. Addictive relationships can even be fatal if a person continues to relapse into one that is physically abusive. There is one bit of good news. In many cases, an antidepressant has helped curb a patient's craving for bad relationships.

Make My Day

Jessie was a 37-year-old male who sought counseling in order to keep his marriage together. Jessie and his wife, Maggie, had three young children, and Jessie didn't want them to grow up in a divorced family as he had.

Jessie was so afraid of divorce that he was turning a blind eye to the affair his wife was having with a man she met at work. Maggie was a secretary, and she would often call home and tell Jessie she was going out after work with others in the office to celebrate different occasions. Those evenings Jessie took care of the children and the house until Maggie got home late. There were other signs, too, that Jessie tried to ignore. Maggie hated for him to touch her, and she took every chance she could to be away from their home. Family and friends tried to make Jessie see the truth. But the more everyone tried to convince Jessie to sever his relationship with Maggie, the more he thought he could fix her. He would say, "I love her so much," or "She isn't that bad," and even, "I'm a Christian, and I don't believe in divorce."

One evening, after getting another phone call from his wife saying she would be home late, Jessie decided to pile the children into the car and drive by Maggie's work. He was there in time to see Maggie leave the office, drive to a nearby apartment complex, and enter one of the units. Jessie then took the children home, fed them supper, and waited for Maggie to come home. When she arrived, Jessie confronted her, and eventually she reluctantly agreed to stop the affair.

Some days later, Maggie called home to say that she was going out with the girls from work for a birthday celebration, and for once it was true. But it set off a chain of events that would prove fatal.

After Maggie left her girlfriends at the restaurant that night, she found her former lover waiting at her car. The man, enraged because she had ended the affair, kidnapped Maggie at knifepoint. He took her back to his apartment and held her prisoner.

At 2:00 in the morning he called Jessie and bragged that Maggie was with him and that they had been enjoying sex all night. Jessie jumped from the bed, dressed quickly, and sped to the apartment, where he found that Maggie's lover had left the door slightly ajar. It turned out that the man had deliberately done so, and when Jessie rushed in, the boyfriend fired three shots. Jessie died there in a pool of blood.

The killer brazenly called 911, and when the police showed up, he told them that Maggie's jealous husband had forced his way in. The man claimed he had shot Jessie in self-defense. That particular state had what's known as the "Make My Day" law, which says that deadly force can be used against anyone who forces their way into a residence. Because police believed the man's claim of self-defense, he was never charged.

Maggie's children, however, were left fatherless, and Maggie herself ended up losing her job and was rejected by family and friends. And it all happened because Jessie relapsed into a destructive relationship. Jessie believed that divorce was not permissible and that only death could absolve his marriage. Sadly, he was right.

The lesson here is that if people we love and trust point out that we seem to be relapsing into a destructive relationship, we should listen and start breaking away. It's the only way not to stay stuck in a relationship with someone who does not reciprocate our feelings.

Top 10 Reasons
We Relapse into Poor Relationships

1. Family upbringing

2. Personality disorders

3. Unaware of our inborn temperament

4. Undetected mood disorders

5. Codependency

6. Shame-based way of life

7. Unresolved anger and bitterness (depression)

8. False forgiveness

9. Financial need

10. Substance abuse

Behavioral Credit Report
and
Donna's Story

Donna had just ended her third marriage and was embarking on her fourth when she heard me on my radio program discussing relapse relationships.

She was already having trouble with her newest relationship and was tired of making bad choices when it came to picking a mate. As a young person, Donna never had the chance to know what a good relationship would even look like. The broken family Donna came from, coupled with a temperament that wanted control and lots of affection, were circumstances that to me indicated she was highly susceptible to relapsing.

I asked Donna if she had ever applied for a loan at her bank. She looked a bit perplexed for a moment, and then said, "Yes, I bought my car and my first home through the bank."

"On what grounds did the bank give you that loan?" I asked. "Did they give it to you based on your good looks? Or because you are so charming? Did the bank give you the loan because you promised to pay it back, cross your heart, hope to die? No? Then they must have given you the loan because you brought them flowers and told them you had an inheritance coming to you from your grandfather. Wait — now I know! They loaned you money because you're a good kisser!"

At this point Donna had heard enough and said, "Of course the bank didn't give me a loan based on all those ridiculous things. They wanted a credit report."

I leaped out of my chair and exclaimed, "A credit report? Why on earth would they want a credit report from such an honest-looking, sweet person like you?"

She said, "They had no reason to believe me. They needed to know I wasn't a con or a liar."

"They would actually think you would lie to them? How dare they!"

That's when I dropped the dramatics and quietly asked Donna, "What criteria did you use when you decided to marry your last three husbands?"

"Well, they were kind, loving, good-looking, and treated me nice," she said. "They were good kissers, and they all told me they loved me."

Suddenly the light went on in Donna's mind, and she realized what she had just said.

"Oh my goodness!" she all but screamed. "I picked my men based on emotions that wouldn't even have gotten me a loan at the bank!"

"Hallelujah!" I said. "You got it."

The way to stop relapsing into poor or abusive relationships is to do a behavioral credit check, regardless of what your emotions say. Act as if you're a banker and your date is a perspective client. After all, you're thinking about loaning this person your body and soul. It only makes sense to do a thorough investigation of who they are, where they have been, how responsible they have been with money, children, and former loves. These are the basic questions to ask; you probably have others that are important to you.

It is crucial that those who are stuck picking the wrong partners learn how to look for red flags and do a behavioral credit report.

Chapter 18

The Battle of the Sexes

Even though young men and women are falling in love each and every day, I have found that one gender really doesn't know that much about the other. And sex education classes aside, there is still an absence of anything in the educational system that teaches males and females how to truly relate to one another. Yet communication problems are one of the main reasons married couples come for counseling. Most men simply do not understand how women really think, and most women do not understand how men think.

The differences in the way genders view things shows up very quickly. Anyone who has observed school-aged children has seen that young boys rarely hold hands, exchange cute little gifts, and scream when they see a mouse. Boys start a trek toward becoming a warrior while girls gravitate toward being a mother. Even though this sounds a bit old-fashioned, I am finding that the fight for women's rights has actually victimized some females, causing them to feel they must punish men. Many of these women who years before were caught up in the women's liberation movement now come to me for counseling, deeply regretting that they disdained men so thoroughly and now have been left to live their lives alone. Many times they admit that they really did wish they had a man to lean on, make them feel safe, and help them through the tough times.

By the same token, I have heard from many a man who took his wife for granted, didn't respect her, and abused her, only to find himself living a lonely, regretful life.

Men need women, and women need men. I believe the more that women are able to act like women — loving, encouraging, responsive, pleasant, giving and nurturing — the more likely they are to get what they need from a man, provided, of course, he is not abusive or abnormal. In the same manner, if a man has learned to act like a real man — providing for the family, preferring his wife's needs over his own, making her feel safe, and standing up for her — any normal wife will be glad to meet his needs.

There are distinct physiological differences in men and women. Creation didn't make a mistake when it built men to work, be invasive and protective and designed women to be soft, gentle and receptive. This is manifested in the sex act, when a man physically enters and impregnates the woman, while the woman receives from the man, incubates it, and gives back to him a gift.

Men create the mood to which women respond. If they give a woman hate, isolation, rejection and abuse, that is what she will incubate and give back to him. Some women bring dysfunctional emotional offspring from former relationships. When that is the case, the woman must learn to receive goodness from the present relationship and not react from the former impregnation of abuse.

The other major problem between men and women is how ignorant they are about the other when it comes to sex. Most men I've interviewed did not have the slightest idea of how women function sexually. And most women didn't have the slightest idea of how men's brains work regarding sex. Both thought that their desires and drives were similar to the other's. Men think women look at other men and lust after them physically, while women think men are turned on by building a meaningful relationship.

Marketing experts know the truth. All you have to do is look at the magazine rack in a grocery store and see the covers plastered with attractive, sensually dressed women. The male brain is attracted by sight, plain and simple. But women too are attracted to the magazines because they want to look attractive like the women on the covers, not realizing they're leading men into a sexual tailspin.

When I ask women about why they want to dress provocatively and look attractive, their answers are a shock to male thinking: "I just want to look that way because it makes me feel good about myself." They also seem to think that men are attracted to them because they are somehow special. They have no idea that men are responding to their innate sexual appetite. When that appetite tells his brain: "Hungry! Need to eat!" then men will flirt and act charming. On the flip side, men actually think women flirt with a man because they're attracted to his physique, somehow sensing that he could make her feel good sexually.

Even though women are attracted to handsome men, they are not thinking sex. Men give love to get sex, and women give sex to get love. While men have an appetite for sex, women have an appetite for love. This causes a big problem in marriages. Once a couple marries, the woman soon finds out that the man wants sex without building on their relationship, which she finds insensitive and selfish. In the same way, the man finds out his wife is not especially attracted to his body and thinks she must be either looking at other men or has become stuck up.

In reality, each sex is only doing what they thought worked while they were dating. But if both can understand and appreciate the other's instinctual needs about sex, they will be much happier. The woman doesn't need to condemn the man for doing what comes natural for him, and men need not condemn women for what comes natural to them.

So what about women who are sexually aggressive? Women who are unable to be monogamous because of an unnaturally high sex drive usually are those who either have a testosterone imbalance or had an abusive childhood. The reason overly sexual women demand more and more affection from their partner is that they're trying to fill an emotional black hole. Theirs is a thirst that is never quenched.

Maria's Story

Maria came to me for counseling after her fourth divorce. She had given birth to three children before her 26th birthday, and all three children had different fathers. Maria told me she loved sex and that all her husbands had eventually pulled away from her after a few short years of marriage.

I said to her: "Maria, since you're coming to me for help, you obviously recognize that there is something drastically wrong with your love life, right?"

She answered with a resounding yes.

"Well, tell me how most of your marital conflicts really started. Did you demand constant physical attention?"

"I hate it when the person, who is supposed to be my lover, works overtime or wants to have time to himself," she said. "I need him to love me, not ignore me." Maria went on to say that she wanted her lovers to hold, hug, and engage in sex with her just about every waking moment.

The first thing I suggested was that Maria get a blood test to see if she had elevated levels of testosterone. When her blood tests showed normal levels, I then had a green light to explore her background.

When Maria was very young, her mother had many men who would come and go in their home. Maria never knew who her biological father was. She soon learned that she could get attention by giving little boys, and big boys for that matter, sexual favors. Like Pavlov's theory of conditioned response, Maria associated sex with love, approval and attention. This started when she was 7. Maria's mother thought it was fine — healthy, even — for little Maria to learn these tricks, telling her she needed to learn what makes men happy if she wanted to get anywhere in a male-dominated world. Operating out of total ignorance, plus her own hurt and abuse, Maria's mother passed on a set of sexually aggressive male behaviors that distorted Maria's normal, healthy needs.

In the same way, men reared with all female influences have come for counseling because they were not able to sustain a relationship. Non-aggressive, sexually passive, indecisive and emotionally sensitive, these men could not fulfill the role that most women needed them to. They said that while women found them easy to relate to at first, eventually their girlfriends wanted them to become more aggressive. I explained that women want to feel safe and secure in raising a family. The truth is, more than one woman has remarked that they would prefer a female roommate to a husband who acts like a woman.

Gender role reversals never quite work out as long-lasting relationships. We must be better educated about gender differences if couples are to avoid getting stuck in their marriage.

Conclusion

Not for Love nor Money

There are girlfriends trying to convince boyfriends to love them. Spouses trying to get the other to cooperate. Parents trying stop a rebellious teen, and friends trying to help a buddy get his life on track.

I've counseled countless couples in which one spouse desperately wanted to save the marriage while the other desperately wanted to leave it. In these cases it was evident that the one who wanted out was willing to lose money, property, family and friends in order to break the connection. No matter what the willing spouse offered, it wasn't enough.

In cases such as these, it seems the more we give of ourselves to try to help those close to us, the deeper we get stuck. I remember hearing my dad say, "Not for love nor money" whenever he was unable to get something to go his way. Usually we can get someone to see things our way by enticing them with love or money. But sometimes, no matter what we do or say, the other person will not change their perspective or behavior toward us. What then?

I believe we continue to stay stuck because we refuse to accept that many times there are circumstances and issues beyond our control. We won't allow ourselves to think that someone near and dear to us may have an addiction, insecurity, a personality or mood disorder, etc.

But if we're going to change our circumstances for the better, if we're going to break free of the issues that are perpetuating a cycle of dysfunctional relationships and behaviors, then we must uncover the hidden issue that is keeping us stuck. A good place to start is with the issues we have addressed in this book.

As adults, whether or not we stay stuck is for the most part our choice. Now that you have read this book and learned some things about the legitimate disorders and personality issues that are keeping you stuck, you have a conscious decision to make. Will you take the steps necessary to become unstuck?

Sources

American Psychiatric Association: *Diagnostic and Statistical Manual of Mental Disorders*, Fourth Edition, Text Revision. Washington, DC, American Psychiatric Association, 2000.

Arno, Richard Gene and Arno, Phyllis Jean: *Creation therapy: A Biblically based model for Christian counseling.* Sarasota Academy of Christian Psychology, 1993.

Carter, Jay: *Bipolar: The Elements of Bipolar Disorder.* Wyomissing, PA, Unicorn Press, 2006.

Goodstein, Ellen: "Unlucky lottery winners who lost their money," Bankrate.com, March 26, 2006.

Thomas, Danny with Davidson, Bill: *Make Room for Danny.* New York, Berkley Book, 1991.

Wikipedia: The Free Encyclopedia. Wikimedia Foundation Inc. Encyclopedia on-line. Available from http://en.wikipedia.org/wiki/.

⌂ Cross**House**

P.O. Box 461592   1-877-212-3022(Office)
Garland, TX 75046   1-888-252-3022 (Fax)

ORDER MORE COPIES OF
Why We Stay Stuck
BY PHONE, FAX or MAIL

Date: Order#:

Bill to: Ship to:

Phone: Card #

                              Exp. date:

Signature:

Item	Quantity	Price	Total
Why We Stay Stuck		$14.95	
Sales Tax (8.25%) Texas Residents Only			
Shipping ($3 for first book, 50 cents for each addtl.)			
Grand Total			